OH! THY NAME IS GOD

KRIMARKA

INDIA • SINGAPORE • MALAYSIA

ISBN 979-8-89277-891-6

Contents

Part 5 Challenges To Evolution Theories

Introduction

It is true that no conclusive evidence can be put forth regarding the existence of God. It does not mean that God is not present. But, He is not visible. So, atheism coexists with theism. Moreover, Charles Darwin's *The Origin of Species*, published in the year 1859, bolstered the views of atheists. Darwin successfully established that living organisms evolved gradually. It took millions of years for organisms to evolve. There are striking similarities among members of a genus from the embryo to the grown-up stage. In fact, there are similarities in the embryo not only among the members of a genus but also among the members of a class as well. Many of Darwin's concepts can never be denied. Only the concepts of evolution cannot provide complete support for atheism. Theories of evolution provide illusory evidence to contest theism.

But despite the views of Darwin, many pieces of evidence are available for the definite presence of God. I have tried my best to establish and cite some examples of the presence of God. Right from the creation of the universe, the initial stage of Earth, revolution and rotation of Earth, how Earth began to rotate and revolve initially, attractive forces between planets and stars, pivotal role of the Sun, presence of atmosphere on Earth, presence of oxygen and carbon dioxide and their utility, mechanism of photosynthesis, mechanism of respiration, heartbeat, seed germination, formation of crude oil, food habits of mankind and animals, how seawater filled up to the current level and who stopped the rains from the seawater engulfing the whole Earth and only occupy 71% of the Earth, how the seawater filled up initially by incessant rains, how the sea level is maintained at an almost constant level, presence of salt in seawater are some of the points elucidated in detail to prove the existence of God. Interestingly, the different faces and fingerprints of almost every individual of mankind, for all the 8 billion people, are explained in detail in the book. These types of variations are almost absent in other living beings. How the ball of fire (Earth) condensed and the surface cooled while the heat is still retained inside the Earth in the form of Magma even after 4.5 billion years is interestingly described. While the surface of the Earth cooled, how the magma pierced through only in some places and by gradual cooling formed mountains while most part of the Earth is covered with topsoil (formation of topsoil is an interesting subject described separately in the book) fit for cultivation. How rivers formed to facilitate cultivation is a topic also covered in the book.

PART 1

ILLUSION OF SPONTANEITY

Universe, Galaxies, and Stars

Of course, the creation of the universe provides us with a definite answer to the presence of God. The theory of the Big Bang is universally accepted regarding the origin of the universe. The Big Bang occurred 13.8 billion years ago. Before 13.8 billion years ago, before the creation of the universe, how much time elapsed with nothing in existence? It is really astonishing to think. Due to the Big Bang, the universe, galaxies, and stars formed. Can we find the reasons and purpose of the Big Bang? Who caused the Big Bang? Where did the hot, dense material come from? Before the Big Bang, what was the position? Without the presence of Almighty God, it is almost absurd to believe that the Big Bang occurred spontaneously. In the universe, 100 billion galaxies have been created. And every galaxy comprises 100 billion stars. Our galaxy, the Milky Way, contains about 100 billion stars. One among the stars is the Sun, around which the planets, including the Earth, the planet we live on, revolve in a regulated manner. It is exciting to think that 100 and 100 billion of stars and celestial bodies have been fixed in a place in the limitless space of the universe without any support! Gravitational forces may have been responsible. But how did the celestial bodies disperse in a regulated manner after the Big Bang and distribute all through the universe? How were the gravitational forces among the celestial bodies balanced with precision so that all the celestial bodies attract or repel one another? These mysteries point the finger to the presence of an omnipotent God who is not bound by time, distance, etc. He is immortal. Before the Big Bang, when a hot, dense material exploded, what was the role of God? Of course, our limited knowledge does not provide an answer. Earth, the solar system, stars, galaxies, and interstellar gas account for 1/6 of the mass of the universe. The presence of dark matter and dark energy may be responsible for the rest of the mass of the universe.

Dark matter may consist of elementary particles created in the Big Bang but not deflected on Earth. Are there gravitational forces working among the celestial bodies of a galaxy? Are gravitational forces acting between galaxies as well? Can we presume that celestial bodies dispersed after the Big Bang and ended up in their present respective positions based on the gravitational forces among them? Another surprising fact is that though the entire solar system had been supposedly created by the Big Bang, the minerals and gases present in the Sun and different planets show huge variations. The Sun consists of hydrogen and helium, both of which are highly combustible. How does the Sun possess these gases in abundant quantity, which is sufficient to last for many billion years? Why are these two gases not found in such large quantities on other planets? Is this a spontaneous act? Certainly, it is in the design of God. Sun, heat, photosynthesis, synthesis of food by plants, and the presence of oxygen, which is the lifeline of living organisms in a significant percentage of the earth, are interrelated and meticulously designed by God.

The Initial Stage of Earth

After the Big Bang, how the hot, dense material which contained dust and gas gathered into a solid hot mass and cooled down to form a planet, Earth, remains an interesting mystery. If we believe it to be a spontaneous occurrence, nothing will stop us from believing so. But the reality is that there must be a supernatural force that created the universe with a purpose. Over time, Earth cooled, causing the formation of a solid crust. How the Big ball of fire began to rotate is another interesting topic. Did the rotation start spontaneously? What has been the external force acting to rotate the Earth all these 4.5 billion years almost at the same speed? Who has provided the initial energy required to rotate the Earth and maintain the force required to rotate the Earth? And what is the purpose of the rotation of Earth? For the sake of day and night? What is the effect if the Earth does not rotate? We will discuss these points in a later chapter. Who has placed the Earth 150 million km from the Sun so that the heat received from the Sun is ideal for the survival of living things? While the hot, dense mass cooled to form the Earth comprising the solid crust, why did the Sun remain as hot stuff that never cooled down and provided the much-needed light and heat that is essential for living things to survive? Earth takes a year to revolve around the Sun in an elliptical orbit covering a distance of 940 million km, which is nothing short of astonishment. What force is acting to regulate the revolution so that the Earth does not slip away from the elliptical orbit but revolves in a regulated manner?

Why and How Did Life Originate On Earth?

How life originated on Earth initially is an interesting topic. How did the first life appear on Earth? Life originated from non-living organic molecules like proteins and RNA? Once the first life came into existence, did they start to evolve in different ways and forms? Who gives life to the bodies so evolved? Body and life are interrelated, and neither can function independently of the other! Is life available on Earth only? Or being available in any other celestial body, which is also an interesting question. When the Earth was formed and existed as a hot, dense mass, no life was available, and it remained in the same state for billions of years. But after cooling down and the sea formed as a result of incessant rains, the first life appeared in the water. The formation of amino acids has been an important turning point in the origin of life. Unicellular organisms first appeared on Earth. The development of the physical structure of organisms by complex chemical reactions is understandable but the most important question is who has provided life to these lifeless organisms comprising chemical molecular structures? For argument's sake, there is nothing wrong in believing the theory of evolution. Simple organisms have evolved into larger organisms, and so on. Unicellular organisms that contain no brain at all have evolved into creatures containing kg of brains that contain countless neurons and synapses to perform a multitude of functions! Is it spontaneous? By evolution only?

Relationship Between Body and Life: From Where Does Life Come? in Which Part of the Body Does Life Reside?

Evolution of living things from the simplest of organisms can be accepted in theory, though divine intervention in evolution cannot be ruled out given the vast variation of living creatures that lived on Earth and became extinct, e.g., dinosaurs and also living creatures now living on Earth. From single-celled organisms, how such a vast variation ranging from tiny creatures to gigantic animals evolved is fascinating! How did the sweet nature of sugarcane and the bitter nature of neem evolve from the same progenitor? Where does the sweet and bitter taste come from? From the soil? Or from the air? How are all these properties coded in the genes of these plants? Have plants and animals evolved from the same common ancestor? Huge variations are seen in the plant kingdom itself, let alone the difference between plants and animals. The evolution of living things from the simplest of organisms is understandable as far as their physical structure is concerned. But where does life come from? A living thing is a combination of both physical structure and life. For every living thing, both physical form and life are necessary for existence. Both cannot exist without the support of another. The physical structure might have evolved and consisted of complex chemical substances, but who created life? A tiny Amoeba has life, and a giant-sized blue whale has life. Who is the creator and custodian of life? Who supplies life to the living things evolved spontaneously without outside interference by natural selection etc.,? Perhaps no answer is available. These questions provide a similar answer that there is a definite presence of God. It is an interesting topic to discuss where life resides. In all cells of our body? Or in some particular cells? We notice that respiration is the key indicator of life or death in animals, including mankind. If respiration stops, death occurs, though in rare cases, respiration can be resuscitated. If life resides in all cells, is life sucked out from all cells before respiration stops? A one-celled Amoeba has one life, and a multicellular, gigantic blue whale also has one life. We cannot precisely pinpoint where and in which part of the body life resides. If the legs or arms of a person get amputated, he does not lose his life. But if a heart, containing tissues comprising many cells, is removed, life is lost. Similarly, if both lungs are removed, life is lost. So is the case with the removal of both kidneys. Death happens only because vital functions are affected and does not mean that life resides in these organs, so life does not reside in any particular cell. Life is independent of the physical structure. But if the only cell present in Amoeba is affected, its life is lost.

Life and The Size of Life

As discussed earlier, there is one life irrespective of the size of the organism. Where does life reside? We cannot pinpoint the exact location of life in a body. In fact, plants have better resilience than animals. In branching trees, such as neem, they will regenerate even if all branches are cut. Trees have no vital organs like animals. Roots are the only important organ of a plant. If uprooted, nourishment and water are cut off, and the plants tend to die. Xerophytes survive long after they are uprooted because they need little water, as transpiration is minimal.

The Pivotal Role of the Sun

The sun gives energy in the form of heat and light. This energy warms and brightens our planet, making the sun vital to life on Earth. The sun is a medium-sized star. Like all stars, it is a huge, fiery ball in space made up of extremely hot gases. The sun is also the closest star to Earth. It is 150 million km away. Even though Earth is really far away, it is the perfect distance from the Sun. Earth lies in the Sun's habitable zone. The Earth is perfectly in the area around a star (The Sun) where liquid water can exist, thereby able to support life. If Earth were closer to the Sun, it would be so hot that its seas would boil away. If Earth were farther away from the Sun, like Neptune, for example, it would be in a frozen condition.

The definite presence of life in other celestial bodies except planet Earth has not been established so far. The Sun sustains all life on Earth. About eight million different species of plants and animals live on Earth. Plants need sunlight to grow. Animals rely on plants directly or indirectly for food. Without the sun, there would be no life on Earth. Food for all living things is synthesised by photosynthesis. By utilising sunlight, plants synthesise food. Plants utilise food for themselves, besides providing succour to animals that are dependent on plants for food. So, the Sun plays a pivotal role in sustaining all life on Earth. The Sun is a storehouse of hydrogen and helium. Hydrogen gets pushed and squeezed tightly into the Sun's core by the strong force of the Sun's gravity. The enormous pressure at the centre of the Sun causes some hydrogen atoms to combine with one another. This process is called fusion and forms helium. Fusion also produces a huge amount of energy, and that energy keeps the Sun burning brightly. The Sun contains trillions and trillions of tonnes of hydrogen and helium.

Where the huge pile of hydrogen and helium came from remains a mystery. After the Sun formed 4.54 billion years ago, a huge quantity of energy and heat has been released into the universe, with the Earth receiving a minuscule percentage of energy and heat, which is sufficient to sustain 8 billion people and billions of animals, besides providing billions of plants with the energy required for photosynthesis. So, no surprise the Sun is worshipped as God in many civilisations such as Aztec and Hindu. But who is responsible for the creation of this God, yes, the God, the Sun? The Sun is a star, a ball of hot plasma, releasing energy by nuclear fusion of hydrogen into helium. Every second, the Sun fuses 600 million tonnes of hydrogen into helium, releasing 4 million tonnes of energy. In fact, the brightness of the Sun increases every million years. The mass of the Sun is so large (radius 695,000 km) that it contains the mass of 99.86 percent of the entire solar system. The Sun will remain so for another 5 billion years. By that time, the entire supply of hydrogen will be exhausted, and the Sun will become a Red giant. With our little knowledge, we presume that all life will become extinct at that time. But who knows how long it will take for God to create another Sun or an entirely different setup in an entirely different manner? Instead of a hot sun, God may create an ice-cool object which may look alike the Sun. This object may emit dark waves instead of light waves! Instead of photosynthesis, a dark synthesis may take place! Living beings that may be adaptable to dark synthesis may be created. Who knows God's plan? Contrary to our belief that the Sun is fixed in a permanent place, the Sun speeds around the Milky Way at the speed of 220 km per second. It takes 240 million years to complete one revolution. So, every celestial object is set in motion. The planets revolve around the Sun. The sun revolves around the Milky Way. Why does the Sun remain hot while the Earth, which remained hot in the initial stages, has cooled down to provide sustenance to life? Is the mystery unravelled? All celestial objects, which are a mass of trillions and trillions of tonnes, hang in the balance without any support, not permanently, but in motion, still not losing the forces that attract or repel each other, thereby maintaining the equilibrium and not falling into fathomless depths in space! Astonishing. The supreme God, whose capacity and wisdom are boundless beyond our imagination, is making these miraculous things happen.

The Sun sustains all lives on earth

Photosynthesis

During photosynthesis, light energy received from the Sun is converted into chemical energy, and the derived energy is stored in carbohydrate molecules. Though the Earth formed 4.54 billion years ago, when photosynthesis first evolved, it is a point for debate. Photosynthesis is responsible for producing and maintaining the oxygen content of the Earth. The evolution of complex life originated after the oxygenation of the Earth. The first photosynthetic bacteria appeared 3.4 billion years ago. Cyanobacteria became the first oxygen producers 2.7 billion years ago. Oxygen is the lifeline of all living organisms. Photosynthesis mainly takes place in the chloroplasts of leaf cells, in which the pigment chlorophyll is responsible for photosynthetic activity. Electrons are stripped from water molecules, and hydrogen combines with carbon to form carbohydrates, while oxygen is released as a waste product into the atmosphere. Of course, the Sun and solar energy have been available since the early stages of Earth's existence; however, photosynthesis might have been a delayed phenomenon. Photosynthesis plays a dual role in the production of oxygen as well as in the utilisation and reduction of the carbon content of the Earth's atmosphere, thereby maintaining an almost constant oxygen and carbon level. An excess of carbon may be harmful, so its content gets reduced and oxygen is produced during photosynthesis, for the benefit of all living things. So, right from the creation of the universe, God is in no hurry at all. Being beyond time and space, He developed every activity step by step, each step taking millions of years and, in some instances, billions of years. First, He created the universe; He created billions and billions of galaxies, created the Sun in the Milky Way, provided the Sun with long-lasting fuel, i.e., hydrogen, and evolved the mechanism of photosynthesis, thereby providing succour to all life on Earth, releasing oxygen, on which most of life is dependent for survival. In fact, oxygen is a waste product in photosynthesis, which is essential for the sustenance of life. With our minuscule knowledge, we realise that life only exists on Earth, while life on any other celestial object cannot be ruled out.

Oxygen

The presence of oxygen, which is essential for life's survival, had not been available, or the quantum available was very minimal, which was 0.001% during the initial stages of Earth. Nitrogen and carbon dioxide were predominant. It took 40 million years between the oxygen-producing photosynthesis and the availability of significant oxygen sufficient for the sustenance of life. The evolution of oxygen is an important milestone that debilitates the spontaneous evolution theory. Anyone can believe the evolution of oxygen is spontaneous. But those 40 million years are crucial for the evolution of higher living organisms. The evolution of oxygen is not spontaneous but one of the important chapters in evolution provided by God. His steps are preplanned and executed in a regulated manner. Oxygen is a colourless, odourless and tasteless gas. Only Earth has a high concentration of oxygen. Mars and Venus contain lower concentrations of oxygen. Oxygen on these planets is produced by ultraviolet radiation of carbon dioxide, whereas oxygen is produced by photosynthesis on Earth. Cyanobacteria, the first organisms to photosynthesise, appeared during the Paleoprotozoic era, resulting in a rapid upsurge of oxygen. Green algae and cyanobacteria provide 70% of free oxygen, and terrestrial plants provide 30%. An adult human being requires 2 grams of oxygen every minute. So, with approximately 8 billion people in the world, the requirement for oxygen amounts to 230 million kilograms every day. The requirement of oxygen for other animals and organisms involving aerobic respiration is not included in this count. Free oxygen was absent 3.5 billion years ago. The gradual increase of oxygen resulted in the Oxygen catastrophe, which occurred 2.4 million years ago. It is called a catastrophe because it was detrimental to, and resulted in the mass extinction of, bacteria which relied on anaerobic respiration. The increased level of oxygen was not conducive to anaerobic respiration, which takes place in the absence of oxygen. Anaerobes were no longer the dominant form; they had to settle in low oxygen environments such as the bottom of the sea. With the increase in the quantity of oxygen, not only did higher living organisms evolve, but also the concentration of greenhouses decreased, and the erstwhile hot conditions changed, giving way to a cool down and resulting in ice ages on Earth. All these are preplanned activities by God.

Oxygen is the lifeline of all living organisms. It is available in the Earth's atmosphere at 21%. This percentage is ideal for the sustenance of life. It is a waste product released during photosynthesis. Oxygen is liberated from the water molecule, leaving hydrogen to form carbohydrates, which combine with carbon dioxide and serve as a source of energy for all living organisms. During the initial stages of Earth, oxygen was almost absent. But as per the pre-plan, God intervened, and the oxygen level gradually increased due to photosynthetic activity, leading to the gradual evolution of life. At one stage, the oxygen level reached 30% before subsiding to the present level of 21%. Oxygen is a component of water, another necessity of life. It is also an important component in proteins, nucleic acids, carbohydrates, and fats. Moreover, it is a crucial component in alcohols, ethers, ketones, aldehydes, carboxylic acids, esters, acids, anhydrides, and amides. In vertebrates, oxygen diffuses through membranes in the lungs and then binds to RBC (Red Blood Cells). Haemoglobin binds to oxygen, changing its colour from bluish-red to bright red. However, anaerobic organisms do not require oxygen. In fact, oxygen is detrimental to anaerobic organisms. As the level of oxygen increased 2.5 billion years ago, it resulted in the Great Oxygenation Event, and almost all anaerobic organisms were wiped out.

Plants' Dependence on Photosynthesis and Dependence of Other Living Things on Plants for Food

Almost all life on Earth depends on a single chemical activity, photosynthesis, for food. It is a perfect arrangement by God. The creation of the universe, the creation of the Sun, the increase in the level of oxygen on Earth, and photosynthesis—the dependence of living things on photosynthesis—are all His preplanned arrangements. These arrangements are necessary for the survival of living things. He has taken each and every step over a long period of time, each step taking a million to billion years. Through photosynthesis, green algae and plants produce food. Carbon dioxide is available in the atmosphere, and water is utilised for photosynthesis. The food produced is stored in the form of carbohydrates. So, plants are not only self-sustaining but also sustain and provide food to birds, animals, etc., which are dependent on plants for food.

In a food chain, herbivores occupy the second position; they eat grass, plants, food grains, etc. Carnivores occupy the third position; they eat small animals, insects, etc., which are dependent on plants for food. Carnivores are not directly dependent on plants and never eat plants. However, they are indirectly linked to plants as they feed on animals and insects, which feed on plants, food grains, etc. Tigers and lions are famous examples of carnivores. Omnivores can occupy the third stratum; they can feed on plants that produce food, feed on carnivores, and can also feed on herbivores. Man is the best example of an omnivore. It is not pertinent to study evolution from the origin of life, but evolution is a continuous process, right from the formation of the universe, the formation of the Sun, the formation of the Earth, the formation of the atmosphere, the evolution of plants, subsequent commencement of photosynthesis, the increase in the availability of oxygen on the Earth's surface, evolution of animals etc., are sequential events.

An abrupt study of evolution from the purview of the origin of life will, of course, drive one to the conclusion that the evolution of organisms is spontaneous and the role of God is difficult to believe. However, events should be linked to the creation of the universe, and with every subsequent development, we realise the presence of God. Why does God not appear directly and show His presence? Invisibility is a boon. We have a tendency to glorify the invisible. We revere our favourite sports star or cinema star as long as we never see them or seldom see them. Suppose we live with our favourite sports/cinema stars, we will no longer revere them, and they will lose their star status in our eyes. So, God decided to stay invisible but make us feel His presence through His deeds. He made some organisms produce food and made some rely on them for food. In fact, food is essential for all. Why has God made food a necessity? He has made food available to other living beings free of cost, while mankind must work hard to obtain food. Initially, food was available to mankind free of cost when the population was minimal and the availability of food exceeded consumption. However, the population explosion made the availability insufficient, and mankind is pressed to find new fields and grow large quantities of food grains. As the population increased considerably, class distinctions among people began to appear, and some individuals abandoned peasantry to become kings, priests, merchants, accountants, soldiers, etc. They found no time to work in the fields and had to purchase food grains at a cost. Over time, those who relied on food-producing people far outnumbered them. The development of mankind from wanderers and food gatherers to the present stage is indeed an interesting topic in the history of humankind. Surely, it is not a divine arrangement but a man-made one!

Food Chain and Food Web

One cannot help but admire the wonderful set-up made by God for providing food to every living being. The rule of one falling prey to another is universal. In every ecosystem, this rule is universally applied. Grass provides food to the grasshopper, the grasshopper falls prey to the frog, the frog falls prey to the snake, and in turn, the snake falls prey to the eagle. In another example, grass is eaten by deer, which then fall prey to tigers or lions. In a pond ecosystem, photosynthetic algae are eaten by small fishes. These small fishes are then eaten by larger fishes, and the larger fishes, in turn, fall prey to birds. Organisms are sequentially arranged through which nutrients and energy are transferred from one organism to another, ensuring the survival of every organism. Too much dependence of all organisms on anything is detrimental and can cause a food crunch. For example, imagine if all organisms depend solely on grass and plants for food, and tigers and lions also eat grass. There would be a severe shortage of food. So, the food chain is beautifully designed by God so that no organism is left to starve for want of food. We can argue that every organism developed its food habits through evolution. Did the shortage of grass compel tigers or lions to turn to non-vegetarianism? Of course, there is plenty of grass for the tiger to eat. Grass-eating deer cannot compete with tigers in eating grass. If such a competition arose between deer and tigers, deer would have died due to a shortage of food, eventually leading to the extinction of the deer species from the Earth. But the food web is so beautifully designed that if at least one species is removed from the food chain, it will result in the extinction of another species that is dependent on the removed species for food. It is our general belief that vegetarian food causes no harm to any other life while non-vegetarians cause cruelty to other living organisms. This is partially true. It is a settled fact that plants also have life. So, no organism can live without causing harm to another organism. We visibly notice the suffering of animals when they are killed, whereas plants suffer invisibly. We cannot always depend on naturally dead plants for our food. So, there should not be a feeling of moral guilt while eating non-vegetarian food. We will have to take it for granted in the belief of God's arrangement in the food chain. But what should be avoided is unnecessary killing and cruelty to other living beings.

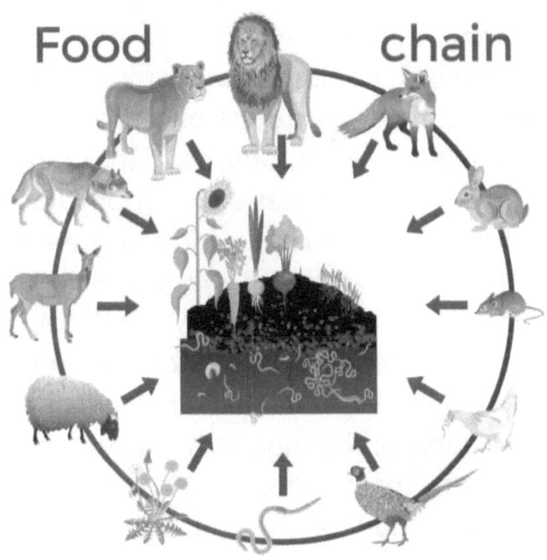

Interdependence of Plants and Animals

Plants power all life on Earth. Plants can survive without animals, but animals cannot survive without plants. Plants are major producers of oxygen, and animals are major consumers of oxygen, whereas animals are major producers of carbon dioxide, and plants are major consumers of carbon dioxide. Carbon in carbon dioxide plays a crucial role in the synthesis of carbohydrates, which are a major source of energy for animals, including mankind, produced by plants during photosynthesis. The world's plants produce a total of 150 billion tonnes of carbohydrates each year through photosynthesis. Plants depend on soil for their nourishment. They consume decayed material from the soil. Plants are consumed by animals for their survival. In turn, carnivores consume the lower animals in the food chain. When living organisms perish, they decompose and form part of the soil, which is again utilised by plants. This is a continuous cycle.

Water: The Elixir of Life

Another important aspect that reminds us of the presence of God is the presence of water, which is very essential for life and can be considered an elixir of life. Water is chemically made up of hydrogen and oxygen, both of which are highly inflammable. But the combination of both is noninflammable and used to extinguish fire! You can attribute complete oxidation to this property, but it is an arrangement by God. Water is present in the Earth's atmosphere in gaseous, liquid, and solid states. While gaseous water plays an important role in the water cycle, water in liquid form is essential for everyday activities, being used for drinking, bathing, and washing. For these purposes, the 8 billion people living in the world need 440 billion litres of water every day, taking a per capita requirement of 55 litres a day. For drinking, every adult human requires an average of 2.5 litres of water. Water is inorganic, transparent, tasteless, odourless, and colourless. It is a fluid present in all living organisms, vital for all known forms of life. In fact, water covers 71% of the Earth's surface, primarily in seas. Most of the Earth is covered by water, with only 29% being landmass. This is a predetermined act of God. We will discuss this further in a later chapter. Why is such a large portion of the Earth covered by water? Without such a large quantity of water, it is impossible to maintain the level of water quantity on Earth. Evaporation of water from water bodies, mainly seas, plays an important role in the water cycle. Water is an important component of every living organism. The human body consists of approximately 60% water. Likewise, all living organisms consist of varying percentages of water relative to their weight. The earliest forms of life appeared in water. Water is required by every living organism for the regulation of body temperature, transportation of minerals, and for digestion. Every metabolic activity requires water. Water is an important component of blood, which is a vital tissue responsible for the conduction of minerals and nutrients to all parts of the body. Almost every activity depends on water. Water is used for navigation, cooking, bathing, and washing. Its neutral nature (pH 7) is helpful in dissolving other elements and forming solutions. Maritime transport is a significant economic activity. All commodities, especially non-perishable commodities, are transported through the sea. Water plays a major role in the world economy. In fact, agriculture, the basic activity that provides food, is entirely dependent on water. Seventy percent of available fresh water on Earth is utilised for agriculture. Fish, which fulfil a major human requirement for protein, are available in large quantities in the sea. How God has interlinked everything in His creation with each other is interesting. Water is essential for photosynthesis and respiration. Salt available in the sea is extracted and used for human consumption. Salt in the sea is formed as a result of sodium and chlorine-washed away in runoff water from land and accumulated over time.

Water Cycle

Liquid water evaporates into water vapour, condenses to form clouds, and precipitates back to Earth in the form of rain. This water cycle has sustained all life on Earth for billions of years. The role of the Sun, which we discussed in an earlier chapter, plays an all-important role in the water cycle. By the heat of the sun, water evaporates from oceans and other water bodies, reaches the atmosphere, cools down at extremely chilly layers of the atmosphere, and precipitates back to Earth as rain. During the early stages of mankind, civilisations flourished on the banks of rivers. For drinking and agricultural purposes, plenty of water is required, which is available in rivers. Mesopotamian civilisation flourished around the rivers Euphrates and Tigris, Egyptian civilisation around the river Nile, the Indus Valley civilisation around the river Indus, and Roman civilisation around the river Tiber. During a later period, cities formed on the banks of rivers, with London being a famous example formed on the banks of the River Thames. God has made resources, including water, available to mankind. However, the pressure of population increase, coupled with reckless use, has made the elixir , water, scarce in some parts of the world. Nearly 1 billion, or 1/8 of the people in the world, lack access to potable water, with a recent example being the people of Iran. Many African countries have been in turmoil for many years due to a lack of sufficient potable water. The United Nations in the year 2015 enshrined Sustainable Development Goals (SDG), with the most important SDG being universal access to safe and affordable water by the year 2050. However, achieving this goal will not be easy, taking into account the geopolitical conditions prevailing in different countries. Water should be used judiciously. Less water-dependent crops must be cultivated. Wheat and rice cultivation require more water compared to millets. Millets require almost a quarter of what these water-intensive crops require. Considering these factors, 2023 was declared the year of millets. To ensure success, people's food habits must be drastically changed. These millets are gluten-free, rich in protein, and rich in mineral content, besides containing minerals essential for health.

Microbes and Fermentation

Every micro organism has its utility.Everything evolved with a purpose under the direction of God.

Fermentation is an enzyme-catalysed metabolic process whereby organisms convert starch or sugar to alcohol or an acid anaerobically, releasing energy. Fermentation comes in four types: Lactic acid fermentation, alcohol fermentation, acetic acid fermentation, and butyric acid fermentation.

1. Lactic acid fermentation:

    Lactobacillus bacteria prepare curd from milk.

2. Alcohol fermentation:

    Alcohol fermentation is used in the industrial production of wine, beer, biofuel, etc. The end products are alcohol and carbon dioxide.

3. Acetic acid fermentation:

    Vinegar is produced in a two-step process. The first step involves the formation of ethyl alcohol from sugar anaerobically using yeast. In the second step, ethyl alcohol is further oxidised to form acetic acid using acetobacter bacteria. It is an aerobic process.

4. Butyric acid fermentation:

    Butyric acid fermentation is carried out by anaerobic bacteria. It is useful in the vetting of jute fibre, rancid butter, tobacco processing, and tanning of leather.

Fermentation is used to produce wine, beer, biofuels, yoghurt, pickles, bread, and sour foods containing lactic acid, antibiotics, and vitamins.

Atmosphere

The atmosphere contains many layers. It is held together by Earth's gravity. Atmospheric density decreases as one moves higher up from the Earth's surface. Without the atmosphere, there is no rain. Without rain, there are no crops. Without crops, there will be no food, and without food, there will be no living beings. So, the atmosphere is created by God and is one of the most important aspects in the sustenance of life.

From 1-12 km from the Earth's surface, there is the troposphere, which contains almost 80% of the total mass of the atmosphere. Cloud condensation, a vital event for life to survive on Earth, takes place in this layer, bringing rain to the Earth. From 12-50 km, the layer is the stratosphere, where atmospheric pressure decreases to 1/1000 of the atmospheric pressure at sea level. Ozone, a modified form of oxygen, is present in this layer, protecting the Earth from harmful ultraviolet radiation. Above the stratosphere, from 50-80 km, the mesosphere is present. The temperature in this layer remains at -70 to -85 degrees Celsius.

From 80-700 km, the thermosphere remains cloudless and free of water vapour. Beyond 700 km and up to 10,000 km lies the exosphere, the outermost layer of the atmosphere where artificial satellites roam. However, the entire mass of the atmosphere is within 100 km above the Earth. The Earth's atmosphere contains 78% nitrogen, 21% oxygen, 1% argon, and 0.04% carbon dioxide. Although the percentage of carbon dioxide in Earth's atmosphere seems negligible, the role of carbon cannot be underestimated. The important product of photosynthesis, carbohydrates, which is the main source of energy, contains carbon. The quantity of carbon dioxide in the atmosphere is increasing due to industrialisation. This increase is responsible for global warming, resulting in the depletion of glaciers, etc. In this detrimental act, there is no role of God, but mankind is entirely responsible. How mankind tends to challenge and manipulate the activities determined by God, particularly in gene modification and Artificial Intelligence, will be discussed in later chapters.

Nitrogen is present in a large percentage of the atmosphere and in a comparatively lower percentage than oxygen on the Earth's crust. Nitrogen, unlike oxygen, seldom reacts with other elements and so accumulates in the atmosphere over time. Nitrogen is very essential for amino acids and proteins, which are the building blocks of life. If oxygen were present in higher quantities in the Earth's atmosphere, the Earth might have burnt, as oxygen is highly combustible. So, the percentages of nitrogen, oxygen, and carbon dioxide at the present level are important for the survival of life on Earth. We may assume this is a purposeful act of God.

Venus has similar physical properties to Earth, but carbon dioxide is present in 96%, and a negligible quantity of oxygen is present. So, the possibility of life on Venus is ruled out in this aspect. The presence of oxygen is high (42%) in Mercury, and as it is very near the Sun, and due to the extremely hot conditions prevailing on the planet, the possibility of life in Mercury is also ruled out.

On the outer planets, hydrogen is present more than any other element. In fact, the percentage of hydrogen is higher in these planets than in the Sun, although the quantity of hydrogen present in the Sun is huge. The Sun has 71% hydrogen, Jupiter (90%), Saturn (96%), Uranus (82%), Neptune (80%). The presence of nitrogen in the atmosphere(78%) makes Earth unique, with only Venus (4%) and Mars (3%) having the next highest percentages of nitrogen present; all other planets have traces of nitrogen or none at all. Nitrogen is essential for plant growth. Analysing the facts, the presence of nitrogen in higher percentages makes Earth unique, much different from other planets. In the presence of the ideal percentage (21%) of oxygen, higher percentages will combust the Earth, and lower percentages will fail to support life, which also makes Earth unique. We may assume that the ideal mixture of nitrogen and oxygen in Earth's atmosphere is an arrangement by God, to support life.

The atmosphere conducts radio waves in the form of electromagnetic waves, and we listen to radio broadcasts. Besides, we watch live telecasts of cricket, football matches, and boxing events. The atmosphere encompasses these properties, and the atmosphere has had this property ever since its formation, but it was only discovered a few hundred years ago. So, the discovery of radio waves provides clues about the presence of God, who has hidden the radio waves in the atmosphere. Humans may discover radio waves, but God is great in providing the radio waves in the atmosphere and providing humans with the knowledge to discover them. In that aspect, every scientist has the blessings of God. They are instruments in deciphering the code provided by God.

Clouds

The formation of clouds is a wonder. Water vapour heated by the Sun does not escape into the atmosphere. If that were to happen, there would be no cloud formation and no rain! Water vapour rises from the Earth but condenses at a certain distance from the Earth and forms clouds. Scientists may assign many reasons for this phenomenon.

A cloud is a mass of water droplets or ice crystals. Water present on the surface of the Earth evaporates due to sunlight. Water vapour enters the air mainly by evaporation. Some of the water from the ocean, lakes, and rivers turns into water vapour and travels in the air. When air containing water droplets rises in the atmosphere, it cools and is under reduced pressure. As the air cools and pressure decreases, water vapour condenses. The vapour becomes small water droplets, and a cloud is formed. The air can hold a certain amount of water vapour in a given area. When a certain volume of air is holding all the water vapour it can hold, it becomes saturated.

If saturated air cools as the atmospheric pressure drops, the air can no longer hold all the water vapour. The excess changes from a gas to a liquid or a solid. This process is called condensation.

The formation of clouds is a wonderful arrangement of God

Rain

Rain plays an important role in the water cycle on Earth. When water on the surface is heated by the Sun, it becomes vapour and reaches the atmosphere to form clouds containing droplets of water. When water vapour in the clouds encounters chilly temperatures prevailing in the higher altitudes of the atmosphere, it precipitates and begins to rain. If water is available on Earth but not cycled, there will be no crops, food grains, or vegetables. So, God has made arrangements for rain, with the Sun, sea, water bodies, and atmosphere playing important roles. Without rain, terrestrial living beings would find it difficult to survive on Earth.

Another important feature is the universal distribution of rainfall except in desert areas. If rainfall is spontaneous and not an act of God, how do all parts of the world receive rainfall? What if it rains heavily in some parts only and some parts do not receive any rain at all? It is difficult to ponder. There will be a heavy rush of populations towards areas of heavy rainfall from areas of scanty rainfall. There will be overexploitation in those areas.

Groundwater

Rainwater

Rainwater falling on the surface of the earth forms perennial rivers which cater to the needs of fields of crops. But river water is not available on all parts of the earth. How can fields in areas not covered by rivers, lakes, ponds, etc. be irrigated? God has made a wonderful arrangement. Groundwater! During the formation of the earth, its surface became solidified and covered by rocks. However, through these rocks, aquifers formed to withhold water that permeates from the surface of the earth. In all parts of the world, groundwater plays an important role in agriculture, besides fulfilling almost 50% of the requirement of drinking water needs of the world's population. But defying God's wish, humans overexploit groundwater, which may result in the depletion of water available in aquifers. This is due to the uncontrolled population explosion. Resources, including water, are becoming scarce in some parts of the world.

Why Not All Mountains on Earth?

When the Earth formed, the high occurrence of tectonic activity and volcanism caused mountains, hills, and hillocks to erupt from the surface. But mountains are not formed all over the Earth; they are limited to only some places. Other parts of the Earth remained as plains, conducive to agriculture. Who has shaped the structure of the Earth? Who has designed the structure of the Earth so meticulously? For rainfall, a certain portion of the Earth has to remain evergreen to enhance and induce precipitation. Mountains, due to their steep nature, are not suitable for agriculture. So, a large portion of forests lies on or adjacent to mountains. For this purpose, God created mountains in limited but sufficient numbers. What happens if all parts of Earth are full of mountains? Farm fields will be scarce, and there will be a shortage of food. God has devised a plan to accommodate mountains and plains in a manner that deems fit for forest coverage and cultivation. Almost all high mountains have dense forest coverage. Trees attract clouds, thereby inducing precipitation.

Importance of the Percentage of Water and Land on Earth

The quantum of water and land available on Earth assumes significance. There is 71% water and 29% land on Earth. Such a large quantity of water is required for the water cycle. Water has to evaporate in large quantities for large-scale evaporation, which is necessary for precipitation. In fact, not a single drop of water is lost in the water cycle, though the quantum of water available on Earth and in the atmosphere may vary at times.

But the interesting question is, how did the water fill up in the sea to the present level? Surely, the water level in the sea could not have reached the present level due to the flow from rivers. Despite the continuous flow of river water into the sea, the water level in the sea seldom increases or decreases. Perhaps, or of course, it was due to incessant rains. Who has caused the excess of rain? Where did the large quantum of water come from in deviation from the water cycle? Who has stopped rain after the sea filled to the present level?

Twenty-nine percent of the landmass is sufficient to feed 8 billion people, which may swell to 10 billion in a decade or two. Who has preplanned this structure? All these questions point fingers to the presence of God.

The formation of mountains only in certain places on earth is an arrangement by God

Why Does Day and Night Occur?

The occurrence of day and night provides us with a glimpse of the presence of God. Every celestial object tends to rotate and revolve. How are they able to rotate and revolve with the large force required? Who provides such a huge force? We may assume that the Sun is attracting the Earth towards it, and the Earth tends to revolve around the Sun. The centripetal force exerted by the Sun and the centrifugal force exerted by the Earth may be responsible for the rotation and revolution of the Earth. But, in fact, the Sun is not stationary but revolves around in the Milky Way. So, nobody can ascertain which force is acting on which celestial body. The only force responsible is the Divine force, which regulates all these activities with precision.

Day and night occur due to the Earth's rotation on its axis in an imaginary line. The Earth rotates from west to east. The portion of the Earth facing the Sun experiences day, while the portion away from the Sun experiences night. The occurrence of day and night is important due to its effect on living beings. If the whole day is full of sunlight, it will disturb the photosynthetic activity of plants. Plants tend to photosynthesise during the daytime and tend to respire at night. During photosynthesis, oxygen is released, and during the night, carbon dioxide is released. This cycle will be disturbed, and even a minuscule change in the percentage of carbon dioxide or oxygen in the atmosphere will have harmful effects.

For mankind, if a day lasts longer than 24 hours, it will not be possible to differentiate between day and night, and sleep, which is essential for recuperation, will be disturbed. Moreover, extreme temperature variations may prevail on Earth. While one part of the Earth, which is not facing the Sun, experiences a chilly climate, extremely hot conditions will prevail in the other part of the Earth facing the Sun. In view of this, God has made the plan perfect. The Earth orbits around the Sun on a tilt of 23 ½ degrees, and this is the prime cause of seasons on Earth. Change of weather conditions is essential for crop rotation. If there is no change of season, crops will wilt either due to extremely cold or extremely hot conditions. There are four seasons: spring, summer, autumn, and winter. Four types of weather conditions prevail in the four seasons. In the northern hemisphere of the Earth, it is summer in the months of June, July, and August. In the southern hemisphere of the Earth, summer prevails in the months of December, January, and February. The seasons are determined by the Earth's relative position to the Sun and the part of the Earth facing the Sun. Due to the Earth's tilt in the axis, in the city of Tromso, Norway, which lies in the northern hemisphere, the Sun does not rise in the months of November to January, and it is night all through these months. In contrast, the Sun rises at midnight in the months of May to July.

Distance of Earth From the Sun

The distance of the Earth from the Sun sets ideal conditions for life to thrive on the planet. The temperature of the Sun is 5778 K (5504°C). The Earth lies 150 million km away from the Sun. The heat is subsidised as it travels from the Sun to the Earth. At this distance, the average temperature of the Earth is maintained at 288 K (15°C), which is neither too hot nor too cold, making the temperature ideal for sustaining life on Earth. The distance of the Earth from the Sun may vary as it revolves around in an elliptical path. But who knows, living organisms that may endure extreme hot or cold temperatures may live on any other celestial body, though nothing is known to us. Only God knows. If we assume that life originated spontaneously on Earth, why is life not present on the moon, the satellite of the Earth, which is approximately 384,000 km away from the Earth? Why has life not evolved on each and every planet, adapting to the conditions prevailing on the planet? Why have living things that can endure the extremely hot conditions in Mercury or extremely cold conditions in Neptune not evolved on the respective planets? No living things are found on the moon. This provides proof of God's action in selecting Earth for the creation of living things and gradually evolving them, endowing brilliance to Homo sapiens, the only species on Earth which has the ability to realise the presence of God, though millions of species have thrived and continue to thrive on Earth. In fact, earlier species of mankind that were extinct, such as Homo erectus, Homo Neanderthal, etc., might have realised the forces of nature like wind, rain, snow, etc., but they perhaps might not have known the presence of God. Of the millions of species on Earth, we are the only species realising the presence of an omnipotent God. Even among the Homo Sapiens, a section of atheists disbelieves in God.

Minerals on Earth

The presence of a variety of minerals is an interesting subject. These minerals are found not only on Earth but also in almost all celestial bodies. But we must come to the conclusion that God has stuffed Earth with abundant minerals for the welfare of living things, particularly humans. Lava, which is still inside the Earth in a hot state, contains more than 2000 minerals. Minerals are found on the surface of the Earth's crust due to the solidification of the Earth's crust. Humans are utilising these minerals for a variety of purposes. Without minerals, almost all economic activity will come to a grinding halt. For example, the latest boom of the software industry requires silicon. By premonition, God has made silicon the most abundant element on Earth, after oxygen.

For construction activity, we need cement, in which calcium is the required mineral present in the Earth's crust at 2%. It is required for the growth of bones in vertebrates. Iron is required in large quantities mainly for construction activity and a plethora of other economic activities, though the availability of iron in the Earth's crust is only 5%. However, sufficiently large quantities, 35%, are available in the magma. Will it be impossible for mankind to extract magma from inside the Earth? Mankind has so far turned the impossible into possibility. With every mineral available on Earth, mankind has made full use of it. For instance, tungsten had been used in incandescent bulbs. Copper, which is the best conductor of electricity, is used for making electrical wires.

Elements with atomic numbers greater than 84 are radioactive elements. Thorium (Atomic number 90) and uranium (Atomic number 92) are found in the Earth's crust and are used for atomic energy. The atomic nuclei of these elements are unstable because of the presence of excess nuclear charge inside them. So, these nuclei undergo radioactive decay to form stable nuclei. Uranium and thorium are found in rock and soil. Thorium has to be converted into Uranium 233 to be used. The isotopes of Uranium and Plutonium, Uranium-235 and Plutonium-239, are used in nuclear reactors. Of course, the availability of Thorium and uranium in the Earth's crust substantiates the view that God has provided these elements for the benefit of mankind, though this is a double-edged sword that can cause havoc if an atom bomb is used.

Lithium is used for making batteries for electric vehicles and lithium deposits are found on Earth. Gold seldom reacts with any other metal and, unlike iron, never rusts, maintaining its sheen for many years and even for many centuries. So, it has a high intrinsic value, and the price is high compared to other metals. God has provided all minerals on Earth. Why has God made humans superior and endowed them with abundant knowledge, almost absent in other species? We will discuss this in a later chapter.

Rocks

Formation of rocks is very important in turning the Earth's crust into a solidified state. As discussed earlier, only God knows how the magma in a hot molten state comprised such a vast variety of minerals. Rocks are aggregates of many different mineral grains, which are fused, cemented, or otherwise held together. Rocks can be classified into igneous rocks, metamorphic rocks, and sedimentary rocks. Igneous rocks crystallised from molten magma. Metamorphic rocks change considerably from the original igneous and sedimentary composition. Metamorphic rock is formed as a result of both heat and pressure or heat alone. Sedimentary rocks form in layers, and they can be distinguished from igneous or metamorphic rocks. Granites are igneous rocks formed by three minerals: quartz, mica, and feldspar. Their crystals interlock as a result of crystallisation during the cooling of molten magma. Classification can be based on the combination of one or more metallic elements, such as sulfides, oxides, carbonates, sulphates, and phosphates.

The mining of rocks for their mineral content has been one of the most important factors in human advancement. Stone tools have been used for millions of years by humans and earlier hominids. The Stone Age was a period of widespread stone tool usage. Stone tools were superseded by copper and bronze tools after innovations in metallurgy, though iron, which is commercially the most important metal today, came into use much later.

Formation of Crude Oil and Coal

The formation of crude oil and coal inside the earth is an act of God for the benefit of mankind. While coal formed as a result of plants and trees submerged inside the earth, crude oil formed from organic material, mainly the dead remains of marine organisms deposited as sediments and formed as a result of high temperature and high pressure inside the earth. The utility of coal, crude oil, and natural gas need not be explained. Coal is used for power generation. Crude oil is used for producing petrol and diesel, which are used for transportation until now, though alternative sources have been found out. The provision of energy from coal and crude oil is an act of God.

Can we imagine human life without crude oil? Without crude oil, transportation of materials from one place to another or from one country to another is impossible. It is also impossible for humans to move from one place to another. Aeroplanes, ships, buses, and motorbikes still rely on petrol and diesel. Crude oil cannot be replenished, and it is mysterious that God has made arrangements for sufficient production of crude oil to last long enough until electricity replaces crude oil for transport. The only mode of travel fully electrified is electric trains. Almost all the trains are run by electricity, except in difficult terrains. Though electricity was discovered centuries earlier, it took time to invent vehicles that are run by electricity. Till then, God had arranged crude oil! A calculated foresight!

Formation of Topsoil and Its Role

In the initial stages of the earth, soil was not formed, but rocks existed. Soil is formed gradually by the disintegration of rocks. It takes centuries for every inch of soil to form. The process of weathering and natural erosion played an important role in soil formation. God has gradually prepared the earth to be viable for plants to survive. Plants supply food to all animals on earth, either directly or indirectly. Rainwater, wind, temperature change, chemical interactions, and the acts of living organisms also play an important role in soil formation. Soil is made up mainly of mineral particles and organic materials. Plants obtain nutrients from the soil. Soil is one of the vital components of our environment and food supply. The formation of soil on Earth has unfolded one of the most important chapters in the evolution of plants and animals Many ancient civilisations, such as the Indus Valley civilisation, buried underneath the soil, are proof of soil formation over a long period. Without soil formation, no food would be available. Though soil formation seems spontaneous, it is an act of God.

A variety of plants grow in various types of soil, including alluvial, black cotton, laterite, mountainous, arid, saline, alkaline, marshy, sandy, silt, clay, and loam soils.

PART 2

HIDDEN TREASURES UNEARTHED - DISCOVERIES AND INVENTIONS

Electricity

The discovery of electricity is an important milestone in mankind's history. In fact, electricity has existed on Earth but was discovered only in the late 18th century. Today, we cannot imagine the world without electricity. Electricity is essential for everyday activities. It is required to light up our homes and streets, pump out water from wells, wash clothes, warm up homes, iron clothes, cook food, and more. Industrially, electricity is used for a plethora of activities, including weaving clothes, producing iron, ginning cotton, manufacturing equipment and utensils, and so on. The discovery of electricity led to the Industrial Revolution, providing large-scale employment to the booming world population. Think of the early times when agriculture was the primary occupation of people. But with the population boom, large-scale employment became necessary, and electricity provided the essential impetus for these developments. With the discovery of electricity, machinery and equipment were invented to run on electricity, and large-scale production started, providing employment to people.

Electronics, though starting as a separate branch, is dependent on electricity for functioning. Without electricity, electronics would not exist. The utility of electronics cannot be underestimated in the present world. Radio, television, and telecommunications are based on electronics. The semiconductor industry owes its existence to electronics. Semiconductors are mainly used in the software industry and are the backbone of computers. The dependence of the modern world on computers need not be explained. Right from the discovery of electricity, electrical equipment, and electronics, God has bestowed scientists with the knowledge to invent them. Human effort is required for any invention, but the blessings of God are essential for any invention. For example Scientists may invent semiconductors, but the invention of semiconductors requires silicon, germanium, gallium and arsenic, which are elements required for the manufacturing of semiconductors. In anticipation of the invention of semiconductors, God has provided these elements already on earth. Scientists can boast of any invention, but God is the driving force behind it.

Until 1600, the existence of electricity had not been discovered. But mankind looked in dismay at the electric shocks given by electric eels. Some scientists made an effort to research the structure of electric eels to find out the cause of the shock. In the sixteenth century, it was discovered that static electricity could be produced by rubbing amber. This is the first tryst with electricity. In the eighteenth century, Benjamin Franklin made extensive research on electricity. However, the orientation of his research was based on lightning. The much-needed impetus was provided by Michael Faraday, who had succeeded in manufacturing a Dynamo, which produced electricity by rotating a coil around a magnetic strip. George Ohm analysed the electrical circuit. Scientists Bell, Edison, Kelvin, Siemens, and Tesla turned electricity, a scientific curiosity, into an essential tool for modern life. Einstein was awarded the Nobel Prize for his research on the photoelectric effect.

Electric current is the movement of electric charge. There are electrical conductors, in which electric current can pass through and electrical insulators, in which electric current cannot flow through. The presence of electrical conductors/ insulators is an act of God. Suppose only electrical conductors are present in the world, and insulators are completely absent; we cannot tap and use electricity for the benefit of mankind. Imagine an electrical switch is made of a conductor instead of an insulator! We cannot switch on as there is a risk of electric shock. So, God has made the world where conductors and insulators exist.

We cannot assume that electricity is only produced when a coil is rotated around a magnet. There are two types of electric current: Direct current and Alternating current. In chemical batteries, we can use Direct current, where the unidirectional flow of current is carried by electrons. An alternating current is a current that reverses direction repeatedly. Edison was a strong supporter of Direct current, while Tesla supported Alternating current. However, the importance of Alternating Current increased. Direct Current cannot be transmitted over long distances, whereas Alternating current can be transmitted over long distances with minimal transmission loss. Electricity cannot be utilised near the site of generation but should be transmitted to far-off places for consumption. Alternating current won the war with Direct current in this aspect. It can be converted into a Direct current at the site of consumption. Massive electricity generation is achieved by converting mechanical energy into electricity using turbines.

Electricity can be generated by Thermal, Nuclear, and hydro generation. Thermal generation is a widely used method of electricity generation. Fossil fuels such as coal are used to heat water, and the steam generated is used to run turbines, which generate electricity. In nuclear electricity generation, heat generated by nuclear fission is used to run turbines for electricity generation. In hydroelectricity production, the mechanical force generated in the fall of water is used to run turbines to generate electricity. Thermal generation heavily pollutes the atmosphere, as hazardous gases are released into the atmosphere during the burning of fossil fuels. The dependency on thermal generation must be reduced by enhancing alternate methods of electrical generation. Nuclear power generation also poses hazards. Safe disposal of nuclear waste remains a vexatious problem. Accidents at nuclear power plants in Chernobyl, Russia, and Fukushima, Japan, taught hard lessons. By comparison, hydropower generation is safe. However, the scope of hydropower production is limited. Alternative renewable sources must be found. Solar energy is an important renewable source of energy. The main problem of the generation of electricity is that it can only be used as it is generated. There is no possibility of large-scale generation for future use. Generation of electricity should be reduced if there is a fall in demand. However, due to ever-expanding industries and increased use of electricity for a multitude of functions, the demand for electricity is rising. Countries such as the USA, China, and India need a huge quantum of electricity. China tops the world in electricity generation, with the high demand being due to production-oriented industries in China. Electricity production is 8 million Gigawatts in the country. The United States of America comes second with 4 million GW, India third with 1.2 million GW, Russia fourth with 1 million GW, and Japan fifth with 0.9 million GW, annually. God provided electricity and its sources of production on Earth. Mankind has made rapid strides in the generation and utilisation of electricity. Electrification in countries such as South Sudan is very minimal, and the world's electricity demand will continue to rise for decades.

Today's common citizens enjoy more comfort than ancient Kings. The discovery of electricity has made the life of common citizens luxurious. The use of cell phones, computers, and the internet has advanced human life to a level that a person living in the previous century could not have dreamed of, even in their wildest dreams.

Invention of turbines played crucial role in the discovery of electricity

Electricity and Economic Development

The modern world entirely depends upon electricity for economic development. Right from lighting homes to heating and cooling homes, a multitude of household activities, including grinding, hulling husk from grains, cooking, and ironing clothes, made work hitherto laborious now comfortable. In agriculture, irrigation had to depend upon cattle to draw water from deep wells. The discovery of electricity and electric motors not only made pumping out water easy but also widened the irrigated area and significantly catered to the ever-increasing food demand due to the population explosion.

The discovery of electricity paved the way for many inventions of electrical equipment, which are beneficial both for domestic and industrial use. Before the invention of electricity, the scope for economic development is very minimal. In many parts of the world, the barter system was in vogue. Essential items were produced manually. Clothes were handwoven. Largescale production of commodities was not common before the invention of electricity. With the invention of electricity and electrical equipment, there has been a boom in economic activity. Today, we cannot dream of the world without electricity. All economic activities require electricity. God provided knowledge to mankind to discover electricity, though belatedly, and it is an important milestone in mankind's history. In fact, God knows what to give, when to give and where to give.

Magnetism of the Earth

Electricity and magnetism represent different aspects of the same fundamental force field. Magnetism and electricity are interrelated. God has provided magnetism inside the Earth. Without a magnet, electricity cannot be produced on a large scale. In order to benefit mankind from electricity, God has made the production of electricity depend on magnetism, which He provided inside the Earth. Magnetism inside the Earth remains in a north-south direction, and like poles repel each other. How did magnetism form inside the Earth? Is it spontaneous? The link between magnetism and electricity is a pre-planned act of God.

PART 3

GOD'S DESIGN OF EVOLUTION

Fruits and Vegetables

The fleshy part of the fruits we eat is mesocarp. The edible part is between the skin (exocarp) and the seeds. The fleshy mesocarp is to save the seeds which lie inside the mesocarp. That is acceptable. But how did the safety mechanism evolve? Furthermore, why is edible mesocarp so delicious? Most of the fruits vary in taste, but almost all are delicious. It is God's design to make fruits edible for humankind, birds and animals. In fact, seeds inside the fruits have been propagated by the animals eating them. God has devised the plan perfectly so that the animals eating fruits benefit as well as the species propagated to far-off places. Thus, the twin objective of the hunger of the animals is satiated, and the species that are propagated are fulfilled. Imagine there is no taste in a mango fruit, for example. There will be no takers for mango fruits, and the fruits will fall beneath the mango tree. There is limited scope for the germination of mango fruits as they will scramble for space and light for survival. Because of their tasty nature, the fruits are taken to various places for eating, and seeds are thrown, which is useful in propagation. Only the mesocarp is made delicious, but not making the seeds delicious is scintillating. What if the seeds themselves are made tasty? They will be eaten along with the mesocarp, and there will be no possibility of mango species to be propagated. The species might have gone to extinction long ago. However, in some species, seeds are also used as edible, such as in legumes. However, as the seeds are produced commercially, people want to cultivate legumes for commercial purposes so the species can survive. But, in legumes, the seeds are as important as the mesocarp, whereas in mango, the mesocarp is large and tasty, and the seed is almost not worth it. The seed is thrown away, which is useful for propagation. In coconut, the mesocarp is worthless, but the endocarp inside is important. Coconuts lack a mechanism for propagation. Though a coconut tree yields thousands of coconuts in its lifetime, all coconuts tend to fall just beneath the coconut tree. But coconut is edible. It contain oil, and humans cultivate it for edible purposes. Why coconut has not evolved for successful propagation is an interesting question. In cereals, the seeds are not protected, unlike in fruits. Wheat and maize seeds are produced in large quantities commercially, so mankind takes care of their propagation. The use of cereals is mandatory, whereas the use of fruits is optional. So, God has taken special care of them for their propagation.

Intervention of God in making fruits as edibles can be observed in their structure

Cereals

Cereals are the main source of energy. Evolution of cereals is not spontaneous but designed by God to fulfill the nutritional needs of mankind and animals. Cereals and pulses account for 70-80% of our energy requirements. Cereals contain carbohydrates and insoluble fibre, cellulose. Proteins account for 6-12%. Fats account for 1-3%. Cereals are a good source of Vitamins A, B, and E. Cereals are the edible seeds of grasses and belong to the family Gramineae. Wheat, maize, oats, barley, millets, sorghum, and rye are cereals. The entire mankind is almost dependent on cereals for food. Cereals provide 376 calories per 100 grams.

The evolution of plants has taken place simultaneously alongside the evolution of animals. Important staple foods of humans are cereals, which belong to the family Poaceae, and pulses, which belong to the family Fabaceae. The plants belonging to these two families almost fulfil the entire vegetarian needs of humankind. They belong to the angiosperms, which are the last to evolve. Today, angiosperms occupy 82% of all plants on Earth. We cannot imagine the consequences if mankind had evolved before the evolution of angiosperms or vice versa.

God is shaping and directing evolution to suit the needs of the relevant epochs.

Wheat

Wheat is an important crop in the world. The chaff is removed, and the kernels are then ground into flour.

Oats

Oats are rich in nutrients, high in fibre, and grown in cold climates. They are not only food but also contain medicinal properties. They reduce cholesterol levels, help lower blood pressure, and are a good source of protein.

Rye

Rye contains more protein than any other cereal. It is a good source of potassium, which plays an important role in metabolism and heart function.

Barley

Barley is one of the ancient grains in human history and possesses medicinal properties.

Sorghum

Sorghum is used as food, syrup, and for making beer. It is gluten-free and contains a small amount of beta-carotene.

Corn

Corn is a good source of protein, Vitamin C, and dietary fibre. Cornflakes, corn chips, and popcorn are made of corn.

Millets

Millets are the staple food of 2 billion people worldwide. Millets are inexpensive. Foxtail, pearl millet, finger millet, and prosomillet are various millets grown all over the world. The year 2023 was declared as the year of millets.

Pulses

Pulses belong to the families Fabaceae and Leguminosae. Chickpeas, lentils, and dry peas are pulses. Pulses are a good source of protein. Almost three times the amount of protein is found in pulses compared to cereals. Nine of the twenty amino acids cannot be synthesised by the body and must come from foods.

Pulses promote the transportation of oxygen throughout the body owing to their rich iron content. They also boost metabolism. Fibres in pulses bind to toxins and cholesterol in the gut and facilitate their removal from the body. Pulses lower the glycaemic index and reduce the risk of diabetes. Pulses are low in fat and rich in fibre, thereby reducing the risk of heart diseases. The antioxidants of pulses possess anti-cancer properties. The embryo of pulses contains Vitamin E, which is an antioxidant.

Pulses contain potassium, which plays an important role in regulating hypertension. Pulses boost immunity and promote T-cell production, which fights against diseases. Soaking pulses in water lowers the phytate content so that the nutrients can be easily absorbed by the body.

Theory of Evolution Vis-à-vis Cereals and Pulses

Pulses release only 1/7 of greenhouse gas emissions per area compared to other crops and can sequester carbon in soils. They can utilise the nitrogen in the atmosphere, thereby reducing the application of nitrogen fertilisers.

The theory of evolution does not provide proof of the adaptation of the digestive system for cereal consumption. Had cereals evolved first, or did the digestive system evolve first? How did the digestive organs evolve? How did the liver, spleen, and colon evolve? Why is the digestive system of cattle different from humans? Why is straw, which is unfit for human consumption, the food of cattle? An elephant, which eats plants in plenty, is physically stronger than mankind. Why were human beings not made adapted to eat leaves and become physically stronger than elephants? In fact, there had been plenty of leaves due to higher forest coverage in primitive times. Mankind destroyed forests to make cultivable lands. Why did mankind not eat grass or leaves and become physically stronger than animals? Every living being has been specifically designed by God. The structure of the hierarchy is such that various species should not compete among themselves for food. A deer should eat grass so that it does not compete with elephants for leaves. Cattle should not eat cereals, so that they need not compete with humankind. Wolves should eat carcasses so that they need not compete with monkeys to eat fruits. The structure is so beautifully designed by God so that various species survive on the planet without hindering the survival of one another.

Attractive Inflorescence, Petals, and Flowers

Why are the petals, flowers, and inflorescence so beautiful? Pollination is important for the reproduction of plants. Bees are important for pollination. God placed honey inside the flowers. To extract honey, bees come to flowers. To attract bees, flowers remain attractive. We cannot assume these arrangements are spontaneous. Can the flowers beautify themselves spontaneously to attract bees? Inflorescence and flowers look beautiful to attract bees. Is it by evolution only?

Attractive inflorescence – By evolution only?

Aroma and Fragrance of Flowers

Not only do flowers look attractive, but they also have aroma and fragrance to attract bees. To ensure double attraction, flowers look attractive besides bearing aroma and fragrance. Pollination is an important activity, providing food to every living being that is dependent on plants for their food.

Adaptations –By Evolution Only?

Bees

God evolved every insect/animal for a specific purpose. Bees are a great example of this. Placing honey inside flowers and the evolution of bees to extract it thereby indirectly helps the plants pollinate. In fact, honey serves no purpose in plants except to attract bees, which helps pollinate them. This is an example of a perfect arrangement by God. We may argue that flowers and bees evolved spontaneously, but this argument does not hold water. Though wasps have great similarities with bees, they are created for different and specific purposes. Bees and wasps belong to the same order, Hymenoptera. They have almost similar types of nests, though the nests of wasps are not as disciplined as bees. They develop similar types of larvae, such as maggots. But they have different food types and aggressiveness. Bees have fur for pollen to gather on. Pollen sticks onto the fur and is carried from flower to flower, which is useful for pollination. Has the fur of bees evolved spontaneously? Why hasn't fur developed in wasps? They have evolved for different purposes.

Porcupine

How quills developed in porcupines as a defence mechanism is a point to ponder. How did quills develop all over the body of porcupines? Why have other rodents not been able to develop quills? Apart from quill erection, the clattering of teeth and emission of unpleasant odour are other defensive mechanisms adopted by porcupines. How did a multitude of defence mechanisms develop in porcupines? Is it by evolution? God has bestowed peculiar characteristics on every living organism.

Why haven't quills evolved in other rodents as in porcupines?

Snake

The presence of venom in snakes is unique. Contrary to our thought, venom is used to kill or subdue prey, though seldom used for self-defence. Venom is a modified form of saliva. Snakes descended from lizards but differ from them in not having legs and in having venom. This bears proof to the fact that evolution is taking place as per the wish of God.

Acacia

The presence of thorns in acacia is another peculiar characteristic. These thorns protect the plants from predation. How did thorns develop? Have the plants themselves developed thorns by evolution? Each individual species is endowed with specific characteristics by God for its own survival.

Tail of Lizards and Limbs of Animals

Though tails form part of the body of lizards and in some species of skinks, in case of emergency, the tail is cut off wilfully to confuse predators. The tail, which is cut off from the lizard's body, wags as if it is another creature. The predator is confused, and the lizard escapes unscathed, leaving the tail apart. How did the lizard acquire this tendency? Have the lizards themselves evolved this feature? Or has God endowed them with it?

However, this unique tendency is not applicable to other creatures or animals. In monkeys, for example, the tail forms part and parcel of the body and will be a handicap if cut off from the body.

Dormancy and Germination
of Seeds

Dormancy and germination of seeds is an interesting chapter provided by God. Seed dormancy is a condition in which seeds are prevented from germination, even under favourable conditions. Seed dormancy may vary from days to months to years. Innate dormancy is a condition in which the seeds are incapable of germination, even if conditions are favourable for the growth of seedlings. The embryo is so immature that it cannot germinate. Enforced dormancy is a condition in which an adequate amount of moisture, oxygen, and light is not available for germination. Induced dormancy is a condition in which the seed has imbibed water, but conditions are unfavourable for germination. Seed dormancy is important in the storage of seeds for later use by animals and man. Seed dormancy is essential for the preservation of seeds during unfavourable conditions. Dormancy allows the seeds to continue in suspended animation without any harm during unfavourable temperatures. Dormancy helps seeds to remain alive in the soil for many years and is a source of new plants, even when all the mature plants have vanished due to natural disasters.

Germination of seeds is a fundamental process in which a seed grows into a plant. During the beginning stage of germination, the seeds imbibe water rapidly, and this results in swelling and softening of the seed coat. Radicle emerges to form a primary root. After the emergence of the radicle and the plumule, the shoot starts growing upwards. Water plays an important role and is an essential source of energy required for seed growth. Besides water, oxygen, temperatures, and light are essential factors that determine the germination of seeds.

PART 4

MIRACLES THAT LOOK ORDINARY

How Do Aeroplanes Fly?

In ancient times, travel and transport were difficult. Mankind tried its best to find ways for easy travel and transport. Mankind has been receiving extra benevolence from God. We will discuss this elaborately in a later chapter. God has already arranged means for easy travel and transport. He has bestowed humans with the knowledge to invent devices to practically utilise this facility. Very early in the 20th century, Wilbur and Orville Wright invented the aeroplane. Subsequent improvements in aeroplanes shrank vast distances of travel so that travel and transport became easy. Thousands of kilometres are covered within a few hours.

Aerodynamic lift is responsible for the flying of aeroplanes. Defying gravity, aeroplanes with tonnes of weight fly in the air. Many theories have been put forth for the flying of aeroplanes. But, God, in order to facilitate easy and speedy travel and transport, made aerodynamic lift possible!

Two important scientific laws explain aerodynamic lift, though these laws were propounded many years before the invention of the aeroplane. The first is Bernoulli's law, propounded by Daniel Bernoulli. The law states, "The pressure of a fluid decreases as its velocity increases and vice versa." Air is fluid, and the law explains aerodynamic lift as a result of the curved aeroplane wing. Air travelling across the top of the wing, which is curved, moves faster than the air moving along the wing's bottom surface, which is flat. Air pressure at the top of the wing is lower, facilitating aerodynamic lift.

Another law that explains aerodynamic lift is Newton's third law. The law states, "For every action, there is an equal and opposite reaction." Air has a mass. The wing's downward push of the air results in an equal and opposite push, resulting in an equal and opposite push upwards. This causes aerodynamic lift. But, both laws do not satisfactorily explain aerodynamic lift.

Doug McLean, in his book "Understanding Aerodynamics: Arguing from the Real Physics," tries to explain aerodynamics. The book includes a section entitled "A Basic Explanation of Lift on an Airfoil," accessible to a non-technical audience. According to McLean, the topic was probably the hardest part of the book to write. He never thought the topic of aerodynamics was satisfactorily explained in the book. His grudge was so great that he subsequently published an article in which he proposed a comprehensive explanation of aerodynamic lift.

Mark Drela, a professor of fluid dynamics at the Massachusetts Institute of Technology, also tried to explain aerodynamics. According to Drela, "If the air parcels flew off tangent to the Airfoil top surface, there would be a vacuum created below them. This creates the area of low pressure atop the plane's wing." Drela himself concedes that his explanation is not satisfactory. Cambridge aerodynamicist Babinski completely disagrees with the views of Drela. John D. Anderson states, "There is no simple one-liner answer to aerodynamics."

Scientists, despite their best efforts, cannot satisfactorily explain how it is possible for the aeroplane to fly. God made flying the aeroplane possible to ensure smooth, speedy travel for the benefit of mankind.

How Do Ships Float?

Ships, which are made of steel and weigh hundreds of thousands of tonnes, float in the water. Astonishing, isn't it? If ships weren't invented, how would we reach the islands? Australia, which is an island continent, could not have been discovered. Transportation of goods, an important economic activity, is carried out through ships. Goods are transported from country to country, continent to continent, via ships. God has made the floating of ships possible for the benefit of mankind. Even a tiny piece of stone sinks in water, but gigantic ships float in water. Amazing! Scientifically, Archimedes' principle explains the floating of ships: "The net upward force on an object immersed in water is equal to the weight of the water displaced by the object." An object floats when the buoyant force is large enough to counter the object's weight. The gravity of the earth pulls the ship down, while the buoyant force pushes the ship up. Both gravity and buoyant force are important. In fact, these are opposing forces. Gravity is not only important for the apple to fall but also responsible for the objects on earth to remain intact. The buoyant force is important for the ship to float. God has created both gravity and buoyant force. The air inside the ship is less dense than water, making the ship float. If water enters the ship and the air is forced out, the ship sinks. The property of ships floating is important for the transportation of huge quantities of goods from country to country. Before and after the invention of aeroplanes, ships are used for travelling from country to country.

Greed for Reproduction of Plants - Food for a Booming Population

Every species has a greed for reproduction. Plants produce a large number of seeds. Every species has greed to dominate the earth. Rice, wheat, and barley grew in the wild in ancient times. Nowadays, they are cultivated in the fields for large-scale production to cater to the food requirements of the ever-increasing population. A single paddy, wheat, or barley plant produces hundreds of grains. It is the species' greed to dominate the earth. But mankind manipulates the greed of the species for reproduction to satisfy the food requirement. It is ironic that mankind has a similar greed for reproduction. However, mankind has adopted measures to control birth rates. Greed for the reproduction of plants is beneficial, while greed for reproduction in mankind has to be channelised, though not to be altogether controlled. Species of plants that are not beneficial to mankind are called weeds. But we call them weeds because their full properties have not been deciphered yet. Mankind has been waging a war with the weeds to eradicate them with little success. Maybe it is God's wish for the weeds to coexist with the beneficial plants. How the plants evolved and how the animals and mankind adapted to eating grains and obtaining essential nutrients is not known for certain. Cows eat hay, and mankind eats grains. Is it by evolution? Or by God's wish? What happens if cattle compete with humankind for grain? Why has humankind not adapted to eat hay? Why are the nutrient requirements of cattle and mankind different?

Why Both Sexes?

Reproduction is the production of a new offspring that resembles the parental generation. Reproduction in plants is both sexual and asexual. But in animals, reproduction is by both sexes, male and female. How is it possible for both sexes to exist in a species? Did they evolve simultaneously? Their reproductive organs are entirely different. Have the reproductive organs evolved spontaneously? Why did only one sex, male or female, not evolve? Without reproduction, a species cannot continue to survive. The lifespan of every species varies, but life is short. If the lifespan is long, living things on earth will scramble for food, water, shelter, etc. So, God made the lifespan generally short. If humans have evolved from apes, how have both sexes evolved simultaneously? The physical structure of both males and females is the same, except for the genitals. How have separate genitals for both sexes evolved? This aspect points the finger to the presence of God, who directs the shape of evolution.

The theory of spontaneous creation cannot explain how the female genitalia is adapted to receive the male genitalia. Did a common genital ever exist? How did two different genitals, both suiting the needs of one another, evolve? This aspect poses a challenging question to evolution. The presence of breasts and nipples in males in rudimentary form provides a clue for the existence of a common sex. So, the intervention of a supernatural force can be guessed. The responsibility of bearing the embryo is entrusted to females. Males had to wander in search of food and bearing an embryo would be an uphill task.

Generally, we know two sexes are present. But, some of the lowest forms of plant and animal life are found to have several sexes. In one protozoan, Paramecium bursaria, there are eight sexes.

Each mating type is physiologically incapable of conjugating with its own type but may exchange genetic material with any of the seven other types.

We know XX chromosomes are present in human females, whereas XY chromosomes are present in males. In plants such as Vallisneria spiralis, Dioscoreasinuata, and grasshoppers, the females have two X chromosomes, while the males have only one X chromosome. The male lacking one X chromosome produces two types of sperms, half with an X chromosome and half without X chromosomes. The sex of the offspring depends upon the sperm that fertilises the egg.

In humans, males have XY sex chromosomes, and females have XX chromosomes. If the X chromosome of a male and the X chromosome of a female pair, then females are born. How the pairing of these chromosomes is so accurate that almost exactly half of the newborns are male or female is not known. It is a divine arrangement. What happens is well understood if the chromosome pairing is tilted in favour of males or females. It will affect sexual balance. Such a wonderful chromosome pairing is not only in humans but also in almost all sexually reproducing living beings. Even after humans have become accustomed to adopting birth control measures, the sexual balance between males and females has not been affected. It is an act of God

In fishes, reptiles, birds, and plants such as Fragaris elatior, the female sex has one Z chromosome and one W chromosome. They produce two types of ova, half of ova carry the Z chromosomes while the other half of ova carry W chromosomes. The male sex has two Z chromosomes. The sex of the offspring depends on the kind of egg, the Z-bearing egg produces males but the W-bearing eggs produce females. Some strange sex determination is present in blue-headed wrasse, a Panamanian reef fish. When the wrasse reaches a reef where a male lives with many females, it develops into a female. When the male dies, one of the females, usually the largest, becomes a male. Within a day, its ovaries shrink, and its testes grow. If the same wrasse larva had reached a reef that had no males, it would have developed into a male wrasse instead of a female.

Temperature-dependent sex determination is present in fishes and reptiles. Temperature-dependent sex determination may have been responsible for the extinction of the dinosaurs, as they were not able to withstand a sudden decline in temperature.

In the slipper snail, all young individuals are male. They turn either male or female depending on the animal's position in the mound. Individuals pile up on top of one another to form a mound. If the snail is attached to a female, it will become male; if removed from attachment it will become female. The presence of a large number of males will cause some males to become females.

How God Balances Both Sexes at Birth

Sexes may reside in different individuals or within the same individual. An animal possessing both male and female reproductive organs is referred to as a hermaphrodite. In plants, where stamens and pistils occur in the same plant, it is monoecious. Organisms in which male and female gametes are produced by different individuals are called dioecious. In short, if separate female and male flowers are on the same plant, it is monoecious. If separate female and male flowers are on different plants, it is dioecious.

Chromosomes 1-22 in humans are called Autosomes. They carry genes for body characterteristics and general physiology. Chromosome 23 in women is XX, and XY in males. An egg fertilised by an X-chromosome-bearing sperm produces a female (XX), and if fertilised by a Y-chromosome-bearing sperm, a male is produced (XY). This is how God balances sex at birth. An equal number of births of males and females have been maintained. What happens if XX chromosomes also exist in males as in females? Only females will be born. Who is the creator of the X and Y chromosomes? It is a mechanism devised by God.

Sperm	Ova 22 A+ X
22 Autosomes+ X sex chromosomes	44 A + XX – Female
22 Autosomes+ Y sex chromosomes	44 A+ XY- Male

So, human male sperm contains 23 chromosomes, 22 Autosomes, and an X or Y sex chromosome. The ova of women contain 22 Autosomes and an X sex chromosome. These two pairs form 46 chromosomes, 44 Autosomes, and 2 sex chromosomes.

Both Sexual and Asexual Reproduction Present in Microorganisms

Both sexual and asexual reproduction are present in Chlamydomonas and Paramecium. Chlamydomonas is a small, unicellular, motile green alga that includes both sexual and asexual reproduction in its life cycle. It reproduces asexually by conidia and sexually by hyphae. Paramecium is a microscopic protozoan that reproduces sexually by conjugation and asexually by binary fission.

Cell

The smallest unit of life is the cell. Every plant and animal is made of cells. Before life appeared on earth, only lifeless elements existed. How did elements combine to form the physical forms of organisms? All organisms consist of elements such as hydrogen, oxygen, nitrogen, carbon, and so on. Who combined these elements and formed the physical forms of living organisms? Did they evolve spontaneously? If so, who gave life to these physical forms? Is life made up of a combination of elements? Certainly not. Here comes the role of God.

The nucleus of a cell carries the hereditary material, DNA, within it. What does DNA consist of? Oxygen, hydrogen, carbon, nitrogen! Almost all humans have DNA made up of these elements. But every individual has varying degrees of intelligence! Who is responsible for this variation? The nucleus is the storehouse of all genetic information. Chromosomes occur in the nucleus. Double-stranded DNA in a chromosome is the genetic material. Chromosome numbers vary from species to species. Every species has a unique chromosome number.

Chromosome numbers in certain species are given below:

- Human – 46 (23 pairs)

- Chimpanzee – 48

- Rhesus monkey – 42

Chimpanzees are genetically related to humans, and the chromosome number variation between them is only two. A higher chromosome number does not mean a higher status. Butterflies have 380 chromosomes, and peppers have 128 chromosomes.

The production of offspring by sexual reproduction is caused by the union of two cells, each with a complete haploid set of chromosomes, and fertilisation causes a diploid phase.

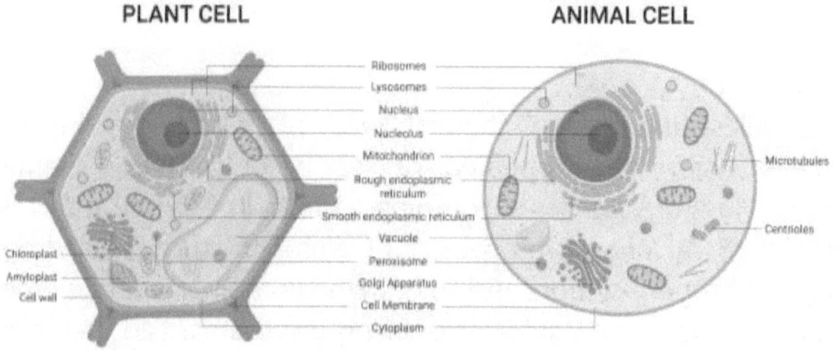

Cell is the basic unit of life

Cell Division

95

Cell division does not stop with the formation of a mature organism but continues throughout life. It is interesting to know that these tiny, microscopic structures have the power to replicate! Is it by evolution? It is estimated that 25 million cells undergo division each second in an adult human. This enormous output of cells is needed to replace cells that have aged or died. Old, worn-out Red Blood Cells, for example, are removed and replaced at a rate of about 100 million per minute. An average adult male has around 36 trillion cells while the average adult female has 28 trillion cells. The largest cell present in the human body is the ovum, 1 mm in diameter while the smallest cell is the sperm cell. Cells are of four types: Epithelial cells, nerve cells, muscle cells, and connective tissue cells. It is difficult to believe these astonishing variations and specialisations of cells and their rate of replication is a result of evolution!

Genetics

Genetics has made valuable contributions to the improvement of food and ornamental crops and domestic animals by applying selective breeding. Seedless varieties of fruits and advances in milk, egg, and meat production of cattle, chicken, and swine have markedly benefited mankind. The Green Revolution and the White Revolution are the principal outcomes of the application of genetic knowledge to agriculture and animal breeding. While mankind cannot create a new species, existing species can be genetically altered for the benefit of mankind. This adaptation is possible only with the gracious consent of God.

Heredity

The tendency of individuals to resemble their progeny is called heredity. Heredity is the process of the passage of characteristics from parents to offspring so that all organisms, including human beings, resemble their ancestors. Heredity establishes the continuity of life forms. "Like begets like." Yet children are not exact replicas of their parents. The offspring may demonstrate many traits not found in either parent. A highly intelligent child may be born to idiotic parents. God measures the good deeds and bad deeds of mankind, which will be discussed in a later chapter. Based on the good/bad deeds of the parents and ancestors, He manipulates the genes of their progeny. It may take one generation or more generations. This is applicable to human beings only. Killing a deer by a tiger is not a sin. But killing a deer by a human being unnecessarily is a sin. Among sexually reproducing organisms, no two individuals have the same heredity. Variation is used by God as the basic material for evolution. Genes are the fundamental units of inheritance. Genetics is one of the youthful biological sciences. Genes are deciphered by God, and He decided to let human beings know the existence of genes. It originated in 1900, with the rediscovery of a scientific article originally published in 1866 by Gregor Mendel, 16 years after his death in 1884. His experiments with garden peas (Pisum sativum) formed a sound basis for further genetic research.

In 1911, T.H. Morgan proposed the theory of linkage. He established the relationship between genes and chromosomes and explained the mechanism of heredity. He was awarded the Nobel Prize. In 1953, Watson and Crick proposed a model for DNA comprising two helically intertwined chains tied together by hydrogen bonds between purines and pyrimidines. Adenine, Thymine, Guanine, Cytosine, and Uracil are purines and pyrimidines.

In 1962, they were awarded the Nobel Prize for the discovery of the double helix model of DNA. God has provided knowledge to human beings to unravel His mysteries.

DNA is the genetic material. It contains Carbon, Hydrogen, Oxygen, and Nitrogen arranged in various combinations. The prerequisite for the creation of an embryo is fertilisation. Fertilisation is the process whereby two sex cells (gametes) fuse together to create a new individual with genetic traits received from both. In plants, the prerequisite for fertilisation is pollination. Pollination refers to the landing and subsequent germination of the pollen on the stigma.

If heredity alone determines the character of an individual, how do siblings have different characters? That is where the effects of deeds of the ancestors are responsible, as narrated in a later chapter, astrology.

Theory of Inheritance

A small seed germinates and grows into a big tree inheriting the properties of a particular species. How are the properties coded in the tiny seeds? A banyan seed develops into a banyan tree and not a neem tree. Likewise, the characteristics of a particular child are coded in the tiny sperm of a male and the tiny ovum of a female. Though the child inherits some properties from their parents, physically and intellectually they are different. A highly brilliant child may be born to highly idiotic parents. A dull child may be born to bright parents. Thomas Alva Edison could not beget another Thomas Alva Edison. Newton could not produce another Newton. Even if a brilliant child is born to a bright parent, the degree of intelligence may vary. A dull child or a bright child may be born to a dull parent. One's good or bad deeds during his worldly life decide the future course of his progeny. But it may take one or more generations for the upliftment or degeneration of progenies. The upliftment or degeneration of progenies is based on the severity of the good deeds or bad deeds of the ancestors. The effect of severe bad deeds continues to haunt us for many generations. A good person has to suffer a bad fate due to serious crimes committed by their ancestors. Thus, not only the traits but also the repercussions of our deeds are passed on to successive generations. A person may escape unscathed for his serious crime in his generation but his successive generation/s may bear the brunt of punishment. A grave crime may be punished in the present generation and continue to be punished in the successive generation/s. Not-so-serious crimes may be punished in the present generation but may not be passed on to successive progenies. God acts steadily but slowly unlike criminal courts which sentence a person for his grave crime within a few months or few years. His progenies will escape unscathed from punishment in courts. But in God's court, not only the accused but also his progenies have to face the trial.

How God shapes the destiny of a child and reveals it through the horoscope and palm? No theory of evolution can explain it. We will discuss this in a later chapter.

Gene Modifications

Humans are able to modify the genes of other plant and animal species. This gene modification is not for the benefit of the species themselves but for the economic betterment of mankind. Genes of wheat have been modified in such a way that the crop yield is higher. Genes of cows modified to give more quantum of milk. Genes of chickens are modified to give more meat within a short time frame. But, the interesting point to note is that humans can modify the genes of a species but cannot create a new species, the role meant for God.

Phenotype and Genotype in Genetics

There are many secrets embedded in genes. Any measurable characteristic or distinctive trait possessed by an organism is called the phenotype of that organism. A phenotype trait may be visible to the eye, such as the colour of a flower. But its genotype may be different. If the colour (phenotype) of a flower is red, the genotype may be either RR or Rr. It is because each phenotypic trait of an organism is caused and determined by at least two Mendelian factors, which are now called genes. Out of these two genes, one gene has been derived from the maternal parent via the ovum and the other gene from the paternal parent via the sperm during fertilisation. These genes may be defined as hereditary units which reside in a long DNA molecule (the main constituent molecule of chromosome) and contain coded instructions or information for the production of proteins, the organic substances which ultimately cause and determine a phenotypic trait in a given environment.

Environment and Phenotype

In the honeybee, Apis mellifera, the difference between the queen and the workers depends on nutritional differences and on pheromones at the larval stage. The flowers of hydrangea may be blue if grown in acid soil or pinkish if grown in alkaline soil, due to an interaction of gene products with the hydrogen-ion concentration (pH value) of their environment.

Mutation and Alleles

Genes are stable and self-replicating structures, but on certain rare occasions, a change may occur simultaneously in them. Mutation alters the coded information of the gene and may result in the production of a defective protein or in the cessation of protein synthesis. The net result is the change in the phenotypic trait. Mutation may change a gene into two or more alternative forms called alleles.

Periodically, a beneficial mutant allele might arise, conferring higher fitness upon its carriers than the pre-existing wild-type allele. This beneficial allele would gradually increase in frequency by natural selection to become the new wild-type allele, while the former wild-type allele would be eliminated. This explains why a brilliant child is born to idiotic parents. This also explains why an idiotic child is born to brilliant parents. It is an act of God.

Linkage and Crossing Over in Genes and Their Importance in Variation

The coexistence of two or more genes on the same chromosome and their inheritance in a group is called linkage. The linked genes do not always stay together because homologous non-sister chromatids may exchange chromosomal segments between homologous chromosomes in a process known as crossing over. Crossing over produces new combinations of genes by interchanging corresponding segments between non-sister chromatids of homologous chromosomes. Linkage reduces the chances of variation within a species, and crossing over increases the chances of variation.

Deletion, Duplication, Inversion, and Translocation of Genes and Their Importance

Loss of a portion of a chromosome (and of some genes) is called deletion. The presence of a part of a chromosome in excess of the normal complement is known as duplication. A rotation of a part of a chromosome or a set of genes by 180° on its own axis is called inversion. Shifting of a part of a chromosome or a set of genes to a non-homologous one is called translocation. All these are of evolutionary significance.

Evolution

Humans have 46 chromosomes, whereas the great apes (chimpanzees, gorillas, and orangutans) have 48 chromosomes. There is reason to believe that humans evolved from a common ape ancestor due to a centric fusion of two acrocentric chromosomes to produce a single large chromosome containing the combined genetic content of two acrocentric chromosomes. It is suspected that structural rearrangement of chromosomes may lead to reproductive isolation and the formation of new species. Still, the great apes survive. However, some genetically modified individuals might have arisen as a new species and began to reproduce, sustaining the new species. This theory vastly differs from Darwin's theory of the appearance and then the disappearance of intermediary varieties and the sustenance of only the new species.

mRNA (Messenger RNA)

Cells in the body create m-RNAs to make specific proteins necessary for the body to function. DNA is a set of cookbooks full of different genes that are used to make proteins. People make about 100,000 different proteins essential for normal function, such as breaking down nutrients and carrying out other important chemical reactions. When cells need one of those proteins, they don't read the recipe directly from DNA. Instead, they make a copy form of a similar molecule, mRNA. Nowadays, m-RNA is a powerful medical tool. The COVID-19 vaccines are the first m-RNA-based medicines. When the vaccines are injected into the arm, m-RNA is absorbed into some of the cells, which read the m-RNA recipe and make the spike protein the virus uses to invade the cells. The body's immune system recognises this protein as foreign and makes antibodies that prepare the body to attack the virus if encountered later. The potential for mRNAs can be used to treat cancer, heart disease, neurodegenerative disease, wound healing, etc.

How Does God Cause Variations and Create New Species?

Non-sister chromatids of homologous chromosomes exchange chromosomal parts. The phenomenon of crossing over is necessary for natural selection because it increases the chances of variation.

As genetic variants arise within a population, the fittest will have a selective advantage and be more likely to produce offspring than the rest. As the fittest continue to enjoy greater survival and reproductive success, new species will evolve.

Skin Colour in Human Beings

A Negro has four dominant genes – AABB. A white has four recessive genes - aabb. If a white marries a Negro, in the first (F1) generation AABB * aabb = AaBb, their children will have intermediate skin colour (Mulatto). In the second (F2) generation, if a Mulatto is intercrossed with a Mulatto, the skin colour of their children will be Negro, coloured between Mulatto and Negro, the colour of Mulatto, the colour between Mulatto and white, and white in the ratio of 1:4:6:4:1 as detailed below in the checkerboard. It is due to polygenic inheritance.

	AB	Ab	aB	ab
AB	AABB 1	AABb. 2	AaBB. 3	AaBb. 4
Ab	AABb. 5	AAbb. 6	AaBb. 7	Aabb. 8
aB	AaBB. 9	AaBb. 10	aaBB. 11	aaBb. 12
ab	AaBb. 13	Aabb. 14	aaBb. 15	aabb 16

Table.1- Negro

Table 2, 3, 5, 9 - colour between Mulatto and Negro

Table 4, 6, 7, 10, 11 and 13 - Mulatto

Table 8, 12, 14, 15 - colour between Mulatto and white

Table 16 - white

Height in Humans

Skin colour in humans is a rather simple example of polygenic inheritance because only two pairs of genes are involved. The inheritance of height is a more complex phenomenon involving ten or more pairs of genes. Thus, out of these 10 or more pairs of genes, an individual having the genotype of more dominant genes will have the phenotype of shortness. (The character of shortness is dominant, and the character of tallness is recessive).

Species-Specific Attraction of Sperms

In many species, sperms are attracted to eggs of their species by chemotaxis. The cell membranes are embedded with receptors that can recognise the chemical gradient. These receptors sense the chemical gradient, and the organism moves in the direction of the attractant. It is convenient for the creation of new species if the sperm of a particular species is attracted by the ovum of another species or vice versa and produces offspring of an altogether new species. But it is not the desire of God to create new species in this way, as it will create species instability and discontinuity. Why hasn't evolution broken this important barrier in the creation of new species?

Rise of a New Species

In fact, reproduction is species-specific. Different species cannot interbreed to produce new species. Members of a species have common characteristics. They are a group of populations capable of interbreeding, and members of a species can reproduce fertile offspring only with members of their own species, not with members of other species. Then how do new species evolve? It may be due to gene mutation, which causes sudden and stable changes in the genes of an organism. Whatever the cause of gene mutation may be, God is directing and supervising such gene mutations

Viruses

Viruses are the simplest form of life. They are intracellular parasites that utilise cellular machinery and energy sources to replicate. As they are not cellular, they are described as 'biological entities' rather than organisms.

Viruses are mostly hostile to mankind, animals, and plants as they cause numerous diseases. But why does God allow viruses to exist? He has granted unlimited power for organisms to reproduce abundantly, yet He also wants to regulate their population growth. However, He has provided knowledge to humans to produce vaccines for controlling viruses as well!

Senses

We know humans have six senses, making them the only species on Earth with such capability. Let us discuss living beings that have only one sense.

Plants and trees have one sense: touch. A climber entwines itself around a nearby support and continues to grow and climb. In fact, they have no eyes to see the nearby support, but their sense of touch makes them aware.

Snails have two senses. Besides touch, they have the capacity to taste.

Ants and termites have three senses. In addition to touch and taste, they have the ability to smell. Although ants have compound eyes, they rely extensively on their sense of smell, whereas most termites lack vision.

Crabs and dragonflies have four senses. Apart from touch, taste, and smell, they have eyes and the ability to see.

Animals have five senses. In addition to touch, taste, smell, and vision, they have ears and the ability to hear.

And mankind has six senses. Apart from the five senses of animals, humans have the capacity for rational thinking.

Though mankind is endowed with a higher status, it also faces the danger of falling into the trap of sin. No other animal, let alone plants, tends to sin. As discussed earlier, unnecessary killing by humans is a sin, whereas killing for food by animals is not considered a sin.

Why is There Pleasure in Sex?

It is not definitively known whether plants experience pleasure during pollination. However, animals derive immense pleasure during sexual activity. Why has God hidden pleasure in sexual activity? God fears that without pleasure, living organisms would avoid sex, leading to a lack of interest in reproduction, and eventually leading to the species being wiped out. Even though there is pleasure in sex, countries such as Japan and now Italy are experiencing negative population growth. People have to be incentivised to have children. It is God's desire for living beings to thrive on Earth. Theorists of spontaneous evolution cannot explain why there is pleasure in sex. This proves the fact that God directs and superintends evolution.

Races of Mankind

Though Homo sapiens belong to the same species, there are different races of mankind. Among these races, Caucasoid, Mongoloid, Negroid, and Australoid are important. The origin of races is a point of debate. As we discussed earlier, there are no identical faces, fingerprints, or corneas for mankind, unlike other species. Why do humans have different faces? It is for the benefit of mankind. People identify one another with the help of facial structure. If all humans looked alike, there would be utter confusion. The presence of different faces in mankind defies the principles of the spontaneous evolution theory. All tigers look alike, all cheetahs look alike, all sparrows look alike, all lions look alike. It is very difficult to distinguish one another based on appearance. If all species evolved spontaneously, why do only the faces of humans differ from one another? Is it due to evolution? Here comes the role of God. Imagine a hypothetical situation. If all humans looked alike, a mother could not identify her son. There are no criminals among lions, tigers, or birds, but among humans, there is no dearth of criminals! The police would find it very difficult to identify criminals if all humans looked alike. According to the theory of spontaneous evolution, all species evolved spontaneously and may continue to evolve. How did mankind get different faces? Different faces mean different facial bone structures. There is nothing wrong with believing in heredity and the inheritance of characters, but God's role cannot be ruled out. Thus, God directs every activity.

According to the theory of spontaneous evolution, humans have evolved from a common ancestor. If the common ancestor were apes, were there races among apes? When did the apes evolve into humans? Why do apes coexist with humans? How was it possible for some apes to evolve as humans and for others to remain as apes? Who is responsible for this evolution? All fingers point to the existence of the omnipotent God. Even if evolution is taking place, God is designing the evolution.

Important characteristics of three different human races are discussed below:

1. Caucasian

   Caucasians have white to reddish-white skin colour, medium to tall stature, narrow to medium-broad faces, light blue to dark brown eyes, linear to lateral body shape, and light brown to dark brown hair. The majority of whites predominantly belong to the Caucasian race.

2. Mongoloid

   Mongoloids have saffron or yellow-brown colour, medium-tall to medium-short stature, medium-broad to very broad faces, brown to dark brown eyes, lateral body shape, and brown to brown-black hair. People from China, Japan, and Southeast Asia belong to the Mongoloid race.

3. Negroid

   Negroids are known for their physical valour. They have black skin colour, medium-tall to tall stature, medium-broad to narrow faces, brown to brown-black eyes, lateral and muscular body shape, and brown-black, woolly hair. Mostly, the people of the African continent belong to the Negroid race.

These variations also occur among animals. African elephants slightly differ from Indian elephants. Evolution may be responsible for these variations. However, nothing evolves in contravention of God's plan.

Hair in Mankind

If evolution is to be believed, millions of years ago, our ancestors were as hairy as chimpanzees and gorillas. Ancient mankind had to toil for food and shelter, and thermoregulation of the body is essential for the loss of heat produced during hard work. So, hair began to diminish, which is helpful in thermoregulation through the evaporative loss of heat via sweating. Plenty of hair may hinder evaporative heat loss. Androgens (male hormones) are responsible for facial hair growth in men, and their absence makes women's faces hairless. Still, the absence of androgens does not affect hair growth on the head genitals, or armpits of women. How did this strange difference in hair growth between men and women evolve?

Most Westerners have no beards or moustaches. They are accustomed to shaving their beards and moustaches. In contrast, Muslims shave their moustaches and grow long beards. Most men have their head hair cut short, and women naturally have no beard or moustache. Is this due to evolution? Will moustaches begin to decrease in Muslims as a result of evolution? Will hair fail to grow on the faces of Westerners (as in the case of women) as a result of evolution?

Various Species of the Genus Homo

Prior to the present Homo sapiens, which is the only existing species of the genus Homo, various species have existed on Earth. God improved every species. Take, for example, the size of the brain. The size of the brain has almost doubled in Homo sapiens compared to the size of the brains of earlier human species. Has the size increased spontaneously? God has not bestowed human beings with brilliance right from the start. Humans have limited longevity and are in a hurry to finish tasks. God's longevity is eternal, and He is not in a hurry. Right from the creation of the universe, He has been acting in a predesigned pattern. Accordingly, He is improving every species. He has a particular preference for human beings.

Some of the salient features of the already existing important species of Homo are discussed below:

1. Homo gautengensis

   This species had big teeth, a small brain, and was only 3 feet tall.

2. Homo habilis

   This species had long arms and had half of the cranial capacity of modern man.

3. Homo ergaster

   This species had a protruding face, lower forehead, and larger cranial capacity than the earlier species.

4. Homo erectus

   This species had a larger cranial capacity of 850 cm^3, showing sexual dimorphism, with males being 25% larger than females, and hunted in coordinated groups.

5. Homo rudolfensis

   They had a much larger brain.

6. Homo heidelbergensis

   They had developed a prelinguistic system of communication.

7. Homo neanderthalensis

   The DNA of Neanderthals differs only by 0.12% from modern humans.

8. Homo floresiensis

   This species survived until 12,000 years ago.

The size of the cranial capacity has been improving to accommodate a larger brain from species to species of humans. If evolution is an automatic process, why can't other species with brains improve the size of the brain, and why is the cranial capacity of only humans improve continually, a mystery?

Speech

Only humans, Homo sapiens, are able to speak. Some animals and birds create different sounds depicting joy, misery, etc., but it cannot be classified as a language. A unique physical structure makes speech possible for mankind. The larynx, located at the top of the trachea, is lower than in other primates. This position increases the range of sounds humans can make. Because of the lowered larynx, food and drink may pass on to the trachea, risking the fall into the lungs if the epiglottis is open. Death may occur. Humans are more vulnerable than other mammals in this aspect.

For speech, the movement of the larynx, mouth, face, tongue, and breath must be synchronised with cognitive ability. However, it is the brain that controls speech.

One bird has the amazing capacity to utter some words. Parrots talk by modifying the air that flows over the syrinx to make sounds. The syrinx is located where the trachea splits into the lungs.

Languages

Subsequent to the development of the ability to speak, many languages emerged in various parts of the world. Language is the most important method of communication. A language consists of a set of words used in a structured way. More than 7,000 languages are spoken all over the world today. English is the official language of 54 countries worldwide. Chinese Mandarin is spoken by the most significant number of people . The country with the most number of languages spoken is Papua New Guinea. However, the number of languages may shrink in the future due to increasing globalisation, leading to linguistic homogeneity. There were 9,000 languages in the world 1,000 years ago, which has now shrunk to around 7,000. By 2050, the number of languages may shrink to 4,500; by 2100, it may further reduce to 3,000; and by 2200, it may shrink to around 100 languages.

PART 5

CHALLENGES TO EVOLUTION THEORIES

Xylem and Phloem

Hyperion is the tallest tree in the world. Isn't it surprising that water reaches the 380-foot-tall tree? How does water reach the top of the tree, defying gravitational pull towards the earth? We may say continuous transpiration occurring in all the leaves of a plant creates a negative pressure in the water column (xylem), and therefore, water ascends to the top of a tree. This exerts an upward pull on the water column, called transpirational pull. The water present in the xylem column transports water up to the tip of the stem and leaves, etc. But we have scientific explanations for the arrangements made by God.

Transpirational pull may be responsible for the ascent of water. However, organic compounds synthesised in the leaves during photosynthesis are transported downwards to other parts of the plant. There is an upward movement of water through the xylem and a downward movement of organic compounds through the phloem. The xylem and phloem are placed side by side, and both the upward and downward movements take place simultaneously. We may narrate and scientifically explain these upward and downward movements. However, the xylem and phloem are arrangements made by God!

Xylem is a dead tissue that contains tracheids, vessels, parenchyma, and fibres. The term "xylem" is derived from the Greek word 'xylon,' meaning wood. Xylem tissue not only transports water and nutrients from the roots to different parts of the plant but also provides structural support to the plant as the xylem contains thick-walled cells and forms the major bulk of the plant body. The cytoplasm is highly reduced, and it only performs the function of conduction. Transportation of water in xylem is unidirectional, upward. The xylem tissues also lack cell organelles; therefore, they are considered dead. Vessel elements in the xylem are analogous to blood vessels. The xylem forms the major bulk of the plant body.

Phloem consists of companion cells, sieve elements, parenchyma, and phloem fibres. The phloem is composed of thin-walled cells and forms the major bulk of the bark. The term "phloem" is derived from the Greek word 'phloios,' meaning bark. Phloem is composed of living cells that transport a water solution of sugars commonly referred to as sap. The sieve elements of phloem are the conducting cells. Phloem is present in dicot roots, leaves, and stems but is absent in monocot plants. In trees, the phloem is the innermost layer of the bark next to the wood. Sieve tube cells are the only living plant cells without a nucleus. Sieve tubes transport synthesised food across the plant. The activities of sieve tube cells are controlled by companion cells.

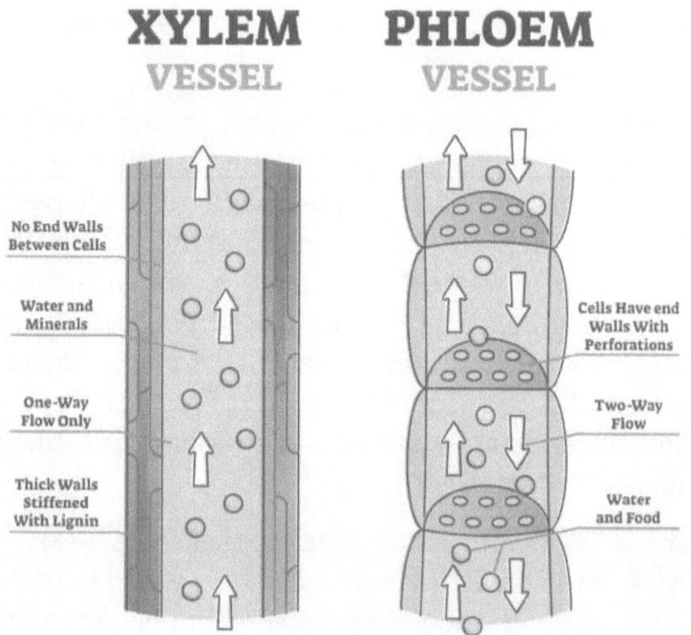

Water is pushed up through xylem defying gravity while the synthesised food is sent both ways through phloem.

Organs of the Human Body and Their Functions

The organisation and functions of our organs are complex. It is difficult to believe they have evolved gradually. Their structure and functions are definite. Let us discuss the structure and functions of important organs of the human body.

Heart

The heart is a fist-sized organ that pumps blood throughout the body. The heart functions as a pump in the circulatory system, supplying blood throughout the body. Blood circulation is performed through systematic circulation and pulmonary circulation. In systematic circulation, oxygen is transported throughout the body and returns carbon dioxide and deoxygenated blood to the heart to be transported to the lungs. In pulmonary circulation, carbon dioxide is exchanged for oxygen in the lungs through the process of respiration.

In the right heart, deoxygenated blood is collected from two large veins, the superior and inferior venae cavae. Deoxygenated blood from the body above the diaphragm is collected by the superior vena cava and emptied into the upper back part of the right atrium. Deoxygenated blood from the body part below the diaphragm is collected through the inferior vena cava and emptied into the back part of the atrium below the opening for the superior vena cava. The deoxygenated blood is pumped to the lungs through the pulmonary artery. Deoxygenated blood collected through two veins is pumped to the lungs through a single artery. What a perfect arrangement! In the lungs, carbon dioxide is exchanged for oxygen in the alveoli.

In the left heart, oxygenated blood is returned to the left atrium through the pulmonary veins. Then, the oxygenated blood is pumped through the aorta, which is a large artery that branches into many smaller arteries, arterioles, and, ultimately, capillaries. In the capillaries, oxygen and nutrients from blood are supplied to body cells for metabolism and exchanged for carbon dioxide and waste products.

The presence of chambers in the heart, each made for specific purposes, defies the theory of spontaneous evolution and the origin of the heart through evolution. There is a presence of two veins, one to collect deoxygenated blood from the body part above the diaphragm and one vein to collect blood from the body part below the diaphragm. It is difficult for the heart to collect deoxygenated blood through one vein, and so two veins have been created. No one can satisfactorily explain how this arrangement is deftly made. Have the theorists of evolution any evidence to prove that there was only one chamber available in the heart initially and other chambers and valves evolved later or there was only one vein in the heart, which collected deoxygenated blood from the whole body and due to over workload another vein evolved to reduce the workload.

The heart pumps 200 million litres of blood in a lifetime.

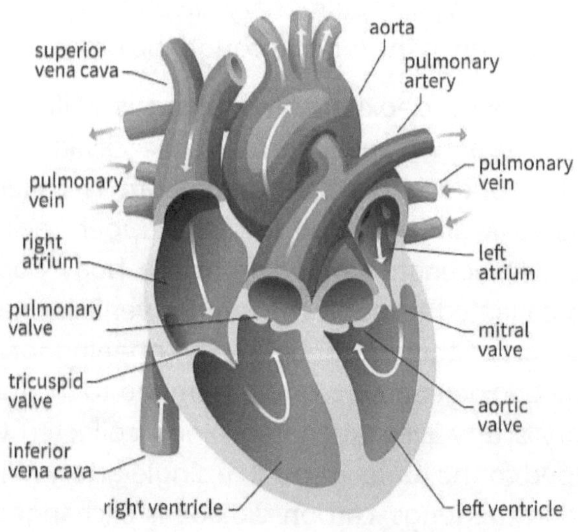

Such a complicated structure of the heart – By evolution only?

Heartbeat

Heartbeat reminds us of the presence of God. Can anyone explain how heartbeat evolved? A heartbeat contains two stages: systole and diastole. In systole, the ventricle contracts, pushing blood into the aorta and the main pulmonary artery. In diastole, the ventricles relax and refill with blood. During systole, the ventricles contract, and the atria are relaxed, collecting blood. In diastole, the ventricles are relaxed, and the atria contract to pump blood to the ventricles.

The heart has its own pacemaker, the Sinoatrial node. Can anybody prove that the pacemaker evolved gradually? Is it not enthralling that the heart, right from its development in the embryonic stage, continues to beat and pump blood throughout the life of a human being? God has created the heart and made it beat.

The sinoatrial node is present in the upper part of the right atrium. In the SA node, an electrical signal is created and travels through the heart, causing the heart muscle to contract. The electrical signal is conducted in a radial way, which cannot be explained by physicians. The lubdub sound is heard during the heartbeat. The lub sound is caused by the closing of the atrioventricular valves during ventricular contraction. The dub sound is caused by the closing of semilunar valves during ventricular diastole.

Humans, mammals, and birds have a four-chambered heart. Arteries carry oxygenated blood from the heart to all parts of the body, getting smaller as they get farther away from the heart. Veins carry deoxygenated blood back to the heart and get bigger as they get nearer to the heart. There are four valves present in the heart: the aortic valve and mitral valve on the left side, and the pulmonary valve and tricuspid valve on the right side. These valves play an important role in pumping blood. The heart beats almost 40 million times in a year. The functioning of the heart defies theories of spontaneous evolution.

Blood Circulation

The cardiovascular system pumps deoxygenated blood, collected from all over the body, from the heart to the lungs for oxygenation. The heart then sends oxygenated blood through arteries to the rest of the body. The main function of the circulatory system is to provide oxygen, nutrients, and hormones to muscles, tissues, and organs throughout the body, and to remove wastes from cells and organs and dispose of them. Deoxygenated blood is collected in the heart's right bottom chamber, the right ventricle, and then pumped to the lungs through the pulmonary artery. Wastes, including carbon dioxide, are expelled from the lungs. Blood cells absorb oxygen inhaled during respiration. Pulmonary veins carry the oxygenated blood from the lungs to the heart's left atrium, and the blood is then pumped into the left ventricle and then out to the body through the arteries. The human body has more than one lakh kms of blood vessels that circulate 1.5 gallons of blood every day. 70% of the body's blood is in veins, 25% in arteries, and 5% in capillaries.

Blood

Blood contains 55% plasma, 45% RBC, WBC, and platelets. RBCs or erythrocytes carry oxygen to all cells in the body. The protein in RBCs is called haemoglobin. Platelets are helpful in blood clotting. There are four blood groups, which are again classified into eight groups based on Rh positive or Rh negative. Rh positive is present in 85% of people, and Rh negative is present in 15% of people. The blood groups are classified based on the presence of antigens on the surface of RBCs. The eight blood groups are detailed below: A(+), A(-), B(+), B(-), AB(+), AB(-), O(+), O(-). No one can satisfactorily explain how the blood groups evolved. Has the blood group O evolved first? Then how did antigens A and B form in human blood? How is it possible for a child to inherit the blood group from the parents?

Blood is formed in the bone marrow. The formation of blood and blood circulation defies the theory of spontaneous evolution.

Do you believe that the earth remained lifeless for billions of years and then elements present on earth combined to form the simplest of organisms in oceans, and evolution took place gradually, leading to more complex forms of birds and animals? Organisms formed structurally from the combination of lifeless elements. If the theory is accepted, who has given life and is giving life to many billion birds, reptiles, and animals? Blood cells in the body are destroyed at a rate of between 3-5 million per second.

Lungs

A pair of lungs carry out the important function of respiration. During respiration, all the wastes, including carbon dioxide, are expelled, and oxygen, which is vital for the functioning of the body and organs, is inhaled. Right from the absence of oxygen in the atmosphere in the early stages of the earth, the commencement of photosynthetic activity, the increase of oxygen in the atmosphere, and the appearance of living beings that depend on oxygen for survival, the maintenance of oxygen levels at an almost constant level (an increase of which is dangerous) depict a clear picture and purpose for which the earth is created. We cannot term it a coincidence. The air is inhaled through the nose, pharynx, larynx, trachea, bronchial tube, bronchi, bronchioles, and then in the alveoli, oxygen is transferred. Though the air contains a higher percentage of nitrogen, it is not utilised but again expelled into the atmosphere. Who has created oxygen and made it crucial for living beings? Why is nitrogen not required? Is it by evolution? Carbon dioxide is a waste product in living beings but is the lifeline of plants, which synthesise food using carbon dioxide. Oxygen is a waste product of plants during photosynthesis, but it is the lifeline of living things required by them for survival. The waste product of one is the lifeline for another! A great balancing act! Is it by evolution? The left lung is smaller than the right lung to make room for the heart. But why is the heart placed on the left side of the chest? Is it by evolution? But the design is made by God.

Respiration

Why is respiration mandatory? Respiration of mankind is made extremely important by God. There is no need for God to watch the good or bad deeds of members of any other species except Homo sapiens. Animals and birds kill or harass others only for food or control of territory. The killing of a rat by a cat or the killing of a deer by a lion is not a sin. In fact, no other member of any species kills or harasses members of the same species as mankind does. Humans, though endowed with much greater brain power than any other member of any species, needlessly harass or kill fellow humans and members of other species. Ancient kings went to the forests, hunted animals, and left their carcasses unattended. Hunting gave them pleasure! Humans are not only endowed with rational thinking but also have enmity, jealousy, vengeance, and cruelty, which almost all other species on earth lack. So, God must watch the good and evil deeds of every member of mankind and record them. How can God watch the good and evil deeds of mankind? Does he possess the network to watch the activities of every human being? Supposedly, He records every activity of mankind through respiration. Oxygen transfer during respiration is a pretext for God to watch the activities of every human being. He has made respiration mandatory for every human being, from birth to death. If respiration stops, He disconnects watching the activities of a human being. He links the activity of a newborn in His Supercomputer and delinks the activities of a man who has stopped respiration and become dead.Living beings are connected with the universe through respiration.

Eyes

A mystery that cannot be solved by the theory of evolution is the functioning of the eyes. The eyesight of nocturnal creatures is greater than in humans. If a human being is locked in a dark room all through his life and permitted to wander in the dark during the night, will his or his progeny's eyesight improve to the level of these nocturnal creatures? In fact, mankind requires more powerful eyesight than the level now available. But greater eyesight during the night will disturb him. A pair of eyes on the backside of the head, apart from the eyes available on the face, would be highly beneficial. A 360-degree rotating eye as in the case of an owl or a compound eye present in the housefly, would be highly useful to man. But this could not happen through evolution. The evolution of the eye remains a mystery. How the lens evolved with such precision is a wonder. The functioning of the iris, retina, and optical nerves is such a wonderful arrangement. God knows the requirements of every species and bestowed them as per the requirement. Though we have a pair of eyes, the picture we see is one. Did the iris and pupil genetically evolve? It captures the picture and sends the signal to the brain. If mankind possesses the vision of a dog, it would be ideal. Dogs can see during the day and also clearly see in the night. Why couldn't mankind evolve such a vision? Dogs have little brainwork like all other animals and birds and need little rest, whereas mankind needs many hours of rest due to higher brain activity. So, vision during the night will disturb his rest. Limited vision in humans is not by evolution but arose due to necessity.

Blinking of eyes is involuntary. Blinking of eyes makes the eyes always wet and removes dust, etc., from the eye. A human blinks 6 million times in a year. Is it by evolution?

Ears

The comprehensive structure of ears defies the theory of evolution. The structure of the ears is created with perfection. When the sound reaches the ears, the eardrum vibrates, and the sound is passed on to ossicles, three small bones. In the inner ear, stereocilia transform the vibration into electrical energy and send it through nerve fibres to the brain. In the inner ear, the cochlea, the hearing organ, processes the sound into electrical energy. The semicircular canals called labyrinthine are responsible for balance. Thus the ears play the dual role of hearing and balancing.

It is difficult to believe that such a complicated organ evolved over a period of time. Though snakes lack outer ears, they can hear through specialised structures in the jaw.

Brain

The brain is the first part to develop in the womb. The composition and functions of the brain defy the logic behind evolution. Humans are physically weaker compared to animals, yet they possess highly developed brains, making them the masters of the earth. Can an elephant imagine shooting a man with a revolver? Can a chimpanzee send a rocket to space? The basic needs of animals are food and shelter; they require nothing more. In fact, humans also need only food and shelter. During early civilisations, mankind needed only food and shelter. However, the brain power of humans developed many things beyond these necessities. His requirements grew beyond food and shelter. He had to travel from place to place, leading to the invention of automobiles. Deposits of fossil fuels are already available on earth. It is as if God expected man to invent automobiles and made fossil fuels to form during the early stages of earth. As movement from country to country was tedious, aeroplanes have been invented to facilitate speedy travel. Before the invention of aeroplanes, ships were invented to travel to far-off countries, islands, continents, and nations where it is impossible to travel by automobiles. The discovery of electricity has been a revelation for mankind. It has already been made available by God, and He endowed scientists with the acumen to discover it with the aim of benefiting mankind. As fossil fuels, such as petroleum, are not replenishable, electric vehicles have been invented, nullifying the fears of automobile shutdown in the event of fossil fuel exhaustion. Why do only humans have super developed brains while the earth inhabits millions and millions of species? Is it a result of evolution? Homo habilis, our ancestor, had half of the cranial capacity of modern Homo sapiens. The cranial capacity of subsequent Homo species continued to enlarge, and the brain became larger and more complex in Denisovans. Modern humans have a brain capacity of 1400 ml, which is larger than in other animals. The evolution of the human brain is understandable. But, the interesting question is why not even a single species has undergone such an evolution of the brain alongside humans? This proves the fact that evolution is shaped by God. To be born a human is itself a blessing, regardless of whether we utilise the opportunity or not. In fact, only mankind can realise the existence of God, and so mankind differs from other species. Will a tiger go to a church/mosque/temple and pray to God? Our closest relatives, the apes, do not have the sense to realise the existence of God. So, humans have a special privilege in the world ruled by God.

Brain and the spinal cord form the central nervous system. The brain is classified into Forebrain, Midbrain, and Hindbrain. Three layers of membranes known as meninges protect the brain and the spinal cord. The skull is very hard and protects the brain. The hardness of the skull again defies the theory of evolution. Can anyone believe that the brain was in the open and as a result of evolution, the hard skull evolved? The brain contains 100 billion nerves that communicate in trillions of connections called synapses, making it one of the largest and most complex organs. Thinking and voluntary movements begin in the part of the brain called the cortex. The brainstem controls breathing and sleep. The cerebellum alone contains 70 billion neurons and is responsible for coordination and balance. The cerebrum is the largest and most important part of the brain, performing functions like interpreting touch, vision, hearing, speech, reasoning, emotions, learning, and fine control of movement.

The brain is composed of 60% fat, 40% protein, water, carbohydrates, and salt. The human brain is four times larger than the chimpanzee brain. The brain comprises only 2% of body weight but needs 20% of the body's blood.

ANATOMY OF THE BRAIN

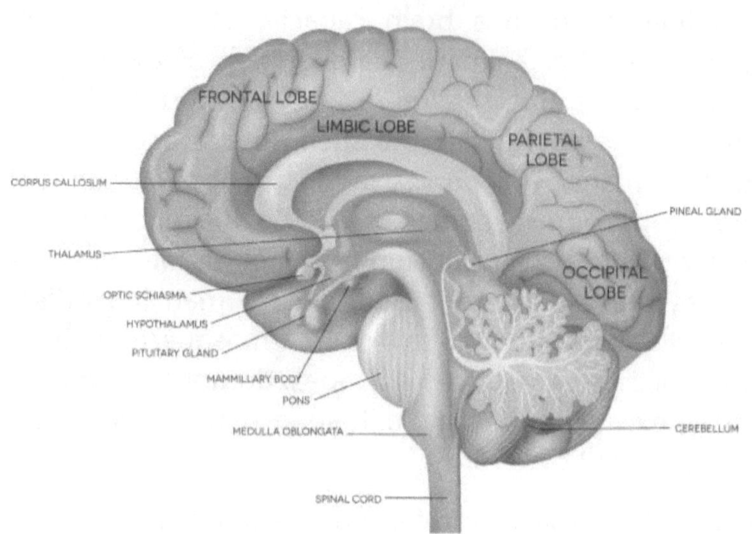

Functions of the brain points the finger to the presence of God

Nervous System

The nervous system is the body's command centre. Originating from the brain, it controls a person's movements, thoughts, and automatic responses. It also controls other body systems and processes such as digestion and breathing.

A vast network of nerves sends electrical signals to and from other cells, glands, and muscles all over the body. The nerves interpret the information and control the response. The nervous system uses specialised cells called neurons to send signals and messages all over the body. The electrical signals travel between the brain, skin, and organs.

Central Nervous System

The brain and spinal cord form the central nervous system. The brain uses nerves to send messages to the rest of the body. Each nerve has a protective layer called myelin, which insulates the nerves and helps the messages get through.

Peripheral Nervous System

The peripheral nervous system consists of many nerves that branch out from the central nervous system all over the body. This system relays information from the brain and spinal cord to organs, arms, legs, fingers, and toes. The length of the nerves in the body is approximately 60 km.

The complexity of the nervous system defies the theory of evolution. How did such a vast network of nerves develop? Is it through evolution? Can we assume that only one or two nerves were present initially and the complex nervous system developed gradually as a result of evolution? It is only an assumption, and no evidence could be produced.

Hands and Legs

Hands are present in some selective species. Hands are highly sophisticated in mankind. Hands are designed by God in such a beautiful way that they are used for a plethora of activities. They are used for eating, cooking, driving, and typing. To understand the utility of hands, take driving, for example. One hand is used for steering the vehicle, and the other hand is used for changing gears. One leg is used for the control of the clutch, and the other leg is used for applying brakes and the accelerator. Will evolution provide one more leg as the right is used for both accelerator and brakes?

Tongue

The tongue is an important organ for eating in most animals. In humans, it evolved as the most important organ for speech. The tongue print is unique to every individual, much like fingerprints. Taste buds in the tongue have a life of only 10 days and are renewed.

Teeth

Humans have 20 deciduous teeth up to the age of 6 years and later develop 32 permanent teeth. The capacity of the jaw is small in childhood and later increases. It seems to be a wonderful arrangement by God, rather than by evolution.

Nose

Primarily created for respiration, the nose is also useful in smelling. However, smelling power has not evolved in mankind to the level of dogs. Dogs can pick up smells that are 10,000 times fainter than the ones humans can detect. If smelling power had been developed to this level in humans, police would not use sniffer dogs to detect bombs and cocaine. God has fulfilled the unique requirements of every species with a unique design.

Fingers

The presence of fingers is a peculiar characteristic. Fingers are present not only in humans but also in apes. The length of each of the fingers varies. In fact, the thumb is different from the rest of the fingers in length and direction. In apes, the thumb is lengthier compared to the thumb of man. In fact, a sixth finger is also present in some individuals, though the utility of the sixth finger is minimal. Imagine the hand is plain and devoid of fingers. You cannot hold a bucket of water or find it very difficult to type on your computer. The shape of the fingers is so finely adapted that man can use them for multiple tasks. Four fingers in the hand contain two joints and three bones, and the thumb has one joint and two bones. The thumb in humans is shorter in length than in apes. Has the length of the thumb been reduced by evolution? Or created in such a way that it is beneficial if it is shorter. Lengthier thumbs will be a disadvantage in humans.

But how can we explain the absence of hands in four-legged animals? Elephants have trunks and use them instead of hands. But giraffes have no trunks. A trunk will be useful for a giraffe to pluck leaves from trees, and instead of trunks, giraffes have a lengthy tongue and a tall neck to pluck leaves from trees. The food of both elephants and giraffes is almost the same, but different types of adaptations are present in elephants and giraffes. A tall neck and lengthy tongue will be beneficial to elephants, and likewise, the presence of trunks in giraffes will be beneficial, but different adaptations are available for both of them. We may infer that every species evolved according to the design of God and was endowed with such capabilities that are necessary for their survival.

Why does mankind have two hands and two legs? Is the presence of more hands and legs beneficial? Animals which have four legs run faster. But why do mankind have only two legs? Given the erect position of mankind, four legs will be highly obstructive. Presume that man has eight hands. It will be highly disturbing to have eight hands while driving ,while working on computers and for every task, two hands are sufficient. And so, God has provided man with two hands and two legs. Has the theory of evolution provided any evidence of the presence of legs and hands, more than two, not only in Homo sapiens but also in earlier species of genus homo.?

Fingerprint Variations

Fingerprints are unique patterns made by ridges and furrows. These patterns are grouped into three distinct types: loops, whorls, and arches, each with unique variations depending on the shape of the ridges.

Loops

Prints that recurve back on themselves to form a loop shape. Loops are divided into radial loops and ulnar loops. Loops account for 60% of pattern types.

Whorls

Whorls form circular or spiral patterns like tiny whirlpools. Whorls are plain, central packet loop, double loop, and accidental loop. Whorls make up about 35% of pattern types.

Arches

Arches create a wavelike pattern and makeup about 5% of all pattern types.

No two people have ever been found to have the same fingerprints -including identical twins. A person's fingerprints remain unchanged throughout his lifetime. The ridge begins to develop during the third month of foetal development and is fully formed by the sixth month.

Of all living things, fingerprints are unique to mankind. There are no dacoits, robbers, or criminals among animals. Except for food, they need nothing. But greed for wealth made mankind prone to sin. Important evidence to find out criminals is fingerprints. As the fingerprint of every human is unique, it is easy to use to find thieves, dacoits, and robbers. So, God made the fingerprint unique for every human being. Facial structure and fingerprints vary for every human being. However, such variations are generally absent among birds or animals. It is not easy to differentiate a sparrow from a hundred sparrows. But it will be easy to differentiate one human being from another among a hundred human beings.

How all elements essential for the formation of the skeleton and flesh of animals are available on Earth is not a coincidence but a planned act of God. For the formation of bones, calcium is required, which is readily available on Earth.

Kidneys

Kidneys are a pair of bean-shaped organs present on either side of the spine. The purpose of both kidneys is the same: the removal of waste, toxins, and excess water from the bloodstream. One kidney is sufficient to carry out these functions, and the presence of two kidneys reduces the workload, ensuring their longevity. The function of the kidneys is to filter the blood, control the body's fluid balance, and maintain the right levels of electrolytes.

All the blood in our body passes through our kidneys 40 times a day. Each kidney has around a million tiny filters called nephrons. Blood enters the kidney, wastes are removed and turned into the urine, and the filtered blood returns to the body. Blood flows into the kidneys through the renal artery, and filtered blood returns to the bloodstream through the renal vein. In the nephrons, the glomerulus filters the blood, and tubules return required substances to the blood and remove wastes.

Is such a sophisticated organ the result of evolution? Can anyone explain how kidneys evolved? Before the evolution of kidneys, how was blood purified without kidneys? All mankind could do in case of kidney damage was to undergo dialysis to purify the blood. We can assume that each organ is a specialised structure created for a specific purpose and not evolved.

Hormones, Enzymes, and Vitamins

Hormones are chemical messengers which are let out in one part of the human body by a gland and being sent to other parts for functions of the body. Enzymes are catalysts that affect the rate of metabolic reactions.

Hormones are useful for digestion, sleep, metabolism, respiration, excretion, reproduction, growth, maintenance of body temperature, and thirst. Enzymes help in the breakdown of proteins, carbohydrates, and lipids. They break down larger molecules into smaller molecules so that the body can use them effectively. Have enzymes evolved over a period of time?

Vitamins are not produced by the body but are required in small quantities. They have to be supplemented through food.

Hormones and enzymes are produced by the body, and vitamins have to be supplemented through food. Why are vitamins not produced by the body? Why didn't evolution take notice of the requirement of vitamins? Who has provided essential vitamins required by the human body in plant and animal food?

Digestive System

Plants, cereals, meat, etc., contain the required nutrients for the body. Our digestive system is adapted to digest and absorb the nutrients required for the body. Is this adaptation a result of evolution? As discussed earlier, rice, wheat, and barley are necessary for the survival of mankind. Hay is sufficient for the survival of cattle. Elephants are vegan, yet their structure and strength surpass that of man. Why don't humans adapt to the food of elephants and gain strength? Is hay poor in nutrition? An ox eats hay and is physically and structurally stronger than man. Have food habits developed through evolution? Why didn't man eat hay and become physically stronger like an ox? In fact, every living being is designed in such a way that each species has unique food habits. All living beings except mankind need no money for food; food is available to them free of cost! They only require effort to make food. Among mankind, wealthy people eat whatever food they want, while the poor struggle for food. The irony is that it is the poor, who are malnourished, have to perform hard manual jobs requiring energy. Malnutrition creates problems for the poor, whereas overconsumption leads to many ailments in affluent sections of society. The affluent seldom perform hard work but have plenty of energy thanks to an energy-rich diet. They have to exercise hard to burn calories, to avoid obesity, which can result in many health complications. Therefore, we cannot conclude that food habits have developed solely through evolution.

Digestion involves turning food into the nutrients and energy the body needs to survive. Solid waste or stool is disposed of through bowel movements.

The mouth, oesophagus, stomach, small intestine, large intestine, rectum, and anus are organs of the digestive system.

Saliva mixes with food to begin breaking it down. When swallowed, the tongue passes the food into the throat and then into the oesophagus. Muscular contractions within the oesophagus, called peristalsis, deliver food to the stomach. The stomach, a container that holds food, mixes it with stomach enzymes. These enzymes break down food for the absorption of nutrients. Cells in the lining of the stomach secrete hydrochloric acid, which kills harmful microorganisms such as viruses and bacteria in the food, and then the processed food is released into the small intestine. The small intestine, consisting of the duodenum, jejunum, and ileum, is a 22-foot-long tube that breaks down food using enzymes released by the pancreas and liver. The duodenum is responsible for the continuous breakdown process of food, while the jejunum and ileum are responsible for the absorption of nutrients into the bloodstream. The leftover food residue, which is in liquid form, passes through the small intestine and then into the large intestine. Solid waste is processed in the large intestine and pushed to the rectum from the large intestine, eventually passing through the anus.

There are glands that secrete enzymes. The pancreas secretes digestive enzymes and insulin for metabolising sugar. The liver secretes bile, which is required for the digestion of fat. The liver also acts as the body's chemical factory and detoxifies potentially harmful chemicals. The gall bladder secretes and concentrates bile secreted in the liver.

Despite mankind having superior brainpower, mankind has one of the ugliest excretory systems of all animals on planet Earth. Cattle, which eat raw grass and hay, contain beneficial bacteria in their excreta. However, mankind, who eat delicious food, have excreta full of harmful bacteria. Why God made the digestive system of mankind so different is a point for debate. Perhaps He wants mankind not to boast of their superiority on planet Earth!

The complex organisation of digestive organs and glands defies the theory of evolution. How is hydrochloric acid secreted in the stomach? Is it through evolution?

How Species Become Extinct

A species is classified as endangered before becoming extinct. There are several reasons for a species to become endangered. Loss of habitat, climate change, and overharvesting by man for commercial purposes is the prime cause of a species becoming endangered. A species may be considered endangered when the species contains only 2500 individuals. In most cases, mankind's actions are responsible for the extinction of species. But, some species defy all attempts by man to make them extinct. Maybe it is God's wish.

Mosquitoes and parthenium are great examples. From time immemorial, mankind is struggling to fight mosquitoes. They are dangerous of being vectors of innumerable diseases in mankind and animals. They are living on earth for almost 100 million years. Mosquitoes belong to approximately 3500 species. Most mosquitoes feed on the plant sap, but female mosquitoes require the blood (especially protein) of the host for the development of eggs. The lifespan of the mosquitoes may be one or two weeks. But they breed rapidly so that their population do not decrease. They use their antenna to detect host odours. Their compound eyes, combined with rapid movement, make their escape easy from adverse situations. The abdomen of a mosquito can contain three times its weight compared to its body weight. Their mouthparts are adapted to pierce the skin and suck blood. Have they evolved or been created? In fact, mosquitoes may make mankind extinct, but mankind cannot make mosquitoes extinct.

Parthenium is a noxious weed that creates allergic respiratory problems. Parthenium is highly toxic to animals and may drastically reduce crop yield as it is an invasive species. They are known for their high fecundity; a single plant can produce 10000 to 15000 seeds. Efforts by mankind to make parthenium extinct have not succeeded. The result is just the opposite. The plant is spreading to new parts of the earth, threatening the fragile species with extinction!

Palmistry

Apes also have hands and palms, but much cannot be interpreted from their palms regarding the character and future of apes. However, in humans, God predetermines the lifetime events of every individual and depicts them through the palms. Most people believe in palmistry. By analysing the structure of palms, the lifetime events of an individual can be deciphered by expert palmists. There are many lines in the palm. At the top of the palm, below the fingers, lies the heart line. The headline is below the heart line, and the lifeline lies around the thumb. The marriage line lies by the side of the little finger. The fate line or money line is the vertical line that starts from the middle of the bottom hand and runs up to the middle finger. Its length may vary. In some humans, the headline is absent, and only the heart line is present in the centre of the palm. Every human born on the planet has distinct and unique lines and mounts on the hand, each conveying specific messages.

Mercury mount is below the small finger. Apollo mount is below the ring finger. Saturn mount is below the middle finger. Jupiter mount is below the index finger. Venus mount is below the thumb. Lunar mount is at the extreme bottom below the small finger. Mars mount is at the centre of the palm. Multiple dominant mounts are considered lucky, and people with raised mounts achieve their goals pretty easily, whereas people with low mounts have to put in extra effort to achieve their ambition. The presence of the fate line is important for a decent career. The absence of the fate line does not mean that the person will not become wealthy, provided the mounts are raised. People in whose hands the fate line is absent, combined with weak mounts, should be extra careful in selecting their career. They should select and pursue a career right from childhood.

However, the lines and mounts depict only the basic structure of one's destiny. Smaller lines continue to develop in the palm throughout life and denote a change of destiny. If people develop a passion for fellow humans and other living things, destiny may sometimes bound to change. A person born into an affluent family is bound to suffer from poverty, whereas a person born into an indigent family can become rich through hard work and perseverance.

Planets and Their Influence in Human Life

Human bodies are made up of physical elements. Planets have their influence on human life because we are all connected in the universe. But it cannot be proved scientifically. Each planet has different gravitational values at the date, time, and place of a person's birth. Accordingly, the impact of each planet on every human life is different. Two children born in a particular second cannot have identical horoscopes. Though the planetary position is the same, the longitude and latitude of the place of birth vary. Planetary positions at the time of birth decide the destiny of a child. But, hard work and perseverance also have their value. Destiny is mostly pre-moulded with a certain degree of flexibility. A person who uses flexibility can alter destiny to certain degrees.

The movement of the planets affords a miniature proof as to how God regulates his task of creation. God creates a body and thrusts the soul into the body. How can the horoscope of a person be interpreted to predict his future? Though man is born on the earth, the impact of the planet Earth is not taken for its influence on a person. But, the Sun, moon, and all the planets and their influence are taken into account. So, a person's horoscope comprises the Sun, moon, Mercury, Venus, Mars, Jupiter, Saturn, Uranus, Neptune, and Pluto. Though Pluto is now downgraded by scientists, though not a planet as of now, it has its role in the horoscope.

The personal horoscope encompasses every conceivable area of life, from birth to death and all stages in between. It reveals your motivations and needs, what drives you to do what you do, where you go, and what you seek.

Astrology is the product of a philosophy that places us inside an ensouled cosmos in which everything is interconnected, and everything has meaning. As such, it stands in contrast to the contemporary view that we are isolated within the universe and that life is a biological accident with no inherent meaning or purpose.

The zodiac was invented by Babylonians, and the movement of planets has meaning as conveyors of divine will. There are 12 signs of the zodiac as the hounding wheels of the horoscope. Apart from the position of the 9 planets, the position of the sun and the moon at the time of birth are drawn in the horoscope. Babylon, Greece, and Egypt excelled in Astrology in ancient times. By the 2nd century CE, horoscopic Astrology became popular in Rome. After the collapse of the Roman Empire, astrology was kept alive by Islamic scholars who translated astrological works into Arabic. Their work was in turn, translated into Latin, eventually finding its way into Europe during the 12th century.

In the medieval and Renaissance periods, every court had its astrologer and astronomer, and even Popes consulted astrologers for advice. For us, most of the time, life might run smoothly, but in times of crisis or uncertainty, it is useful to have a tool that allows you to glimpse underneath the surface to see what might be going on at a deeper level. Astrology is useful for forecasting not only future events but also the path you have to take in order to reduce/avoid misfortunes that may befall if corrective steps are not taken.

As the earth takes 24 hours to spin around its axis, all the 12 zodiac signs will rise on the eastern horizon. So, in a day, there will be 12 ascendants. Hence 24 hours divided by 12 = 2 hours is the span of each ascendant. Each sign has 30 degrees (360/12). There are 27 stars associated with these 12 ascendants. These 27 stars are again divided by 4 parts, padas 1, 2, 3, 4 altogether, making 108 star padas in a day. So, a person's horoscope is determined by the latitude and longitude of the place of birth and the ascendant, the planetary position, the position of the sun and the moon. This makes every person's horoscope unique. Ascendant is determined based on the exact time, date, and place of birth. The rising sign on the eastern horizon at the moment of birth becomes the ascendant. So, two humans born at the same time but in different places can have different ascendants.

The position of the moon assumes significance in a horoscope as the moon represents the mind. The ascendant completes the 27 stars and 108 star padas in a day. The ascendant (1st house) and the house of the moon are influential factors in a person's life. The ascendant can be better described as the very first moment of contact between the soul and its new life on earth.

A horoscope is divided into 12 houses, and each house forms a 120-degree angle with the other. The moment an individual is born, the position of the planets in the specific houses influences various traits in the person's life.

Zodiac signs and ruling planets

Zodiac sign	Ruling planet
1) Aries	Mars
2) Taurus	Venus
3) Gemini	Mercury
4) Cancer	Moon
5) Leo	Sun
6) Virgo	Mercury
7) Libra	Venus
8) Scorpio	Mars
9) Sagittarius	Jupiter
10) Capricorn	Saturn
11) Aquarius	Saturn
12) Pisces	Jupiter

Some planets are natural friends to certain other planets. The placement of one planet from another planet in an individual horoscope creates a temporary relationship. But friends can be enemies and enemies can be friends in certain circumstances. Sun and Saturn are enemies, but they may become friends. Sun and Jupiter are friends, but they may become enemies based on a particular position between the two planets, and friendship and enmity may cease when the position changes.

Planets	Friends	Enemies	Neutral
Sun	Moon Mars Jupiter	Venus Saturn	Mercury
Moon	Sun Mercury	--------	Jupiter Mars Saturn Venus
Mars	Sun Moon Jupiter	Mercury	Saturn Venus
Mercury	Sun Venus	Moon	Mars Jupiter Saturn
Jupiter	Sun Moon Mars	Venus Mercury	Saturn
Venus	Mercury Saturn	Sun Moon	Mars Jupiter
Saturn	Mercury Venus	Sun Moon Mars	Jupiter

How a combination of planets in a house work?

Friend+ friend=great friend

Friend+ neutral=friend

Friend+ enemy=neutral

Enemy+ neutral=Enemy

Enemy+ Enemy= Bitter enemy

The constellation of 27 fixed stars are situated far off from the planets and make up the 12 Zodiac signs. The whole planetary system is almost similar to that of a Government.

Sun - King

Moon - Queen

Mars - Commander in chief

Mercury - Prince

Jupiter - Minister in religious matter

Venus - Minister in politics

Saturn - Servant

Saturn is the dispenser of justice, obeying orders from His Lord, God, and so he is a servant of God.

The birth sign is most important in a horoscope, and future predictions of a horoscope are built on the stability of the birth sign.

Period of stay of the planets in Zodiac signs

Moon - stays 2 1/4 days at the rate of one star every day.

Sun, Mercury, and Venus - Stay for a month

Mars - stays for 1 ½ months

Jupiter - stays for one year

Saturn - stays for 2 ½ years.

Transit of Jupiter and Saturn from one zodiac sign to another is of great importance and likely to affect a person's fortunes. Planets except the Sun and Moon have retrograde motions when they come in proximity to the Sun. In such cases, the period of stay in a zodiac sign is prolonged. The period of stay is based on the distance of the planets from the earth. As the distance of the planets from the earth becomes greater, the circumference of their movements or the length of their orbit also becomes greater. Hence, some planets require a longer time than others in their revolution. The Moon is the nearest celestial object and so changes from one Zodiac sign to another in 2 ¼ days, whereas Saturn, which is a far-off planet, takes approximately 2 1/2 years to transition from zodiac signs.

When Saturn occupies the 12th, 1st, or 2nd zodiac sign in the current transit, taking into account the relative zodiac sign of the moon in the birth chart, the 7 ½ years (2 ½ years * 3 zodiac signs) period is tumultuous for most people especially in the first cycle of transit of their lifetime. The Saturn approximately takes 30 years to complete one cycle (2 ½ years * 12 Zodiac signs). The Saturn in the 8th zodiac sign in the current transit, from the zodiac sign of the moon in a birth chart, is not welcome. That is why the transit of Saturn assumes significance.

Days are named after the planets.

Sunday - Sun

Monday - Moon

Tuesday - Mars

Wednesday - Mercury

Thursday - Jupiter

Friday - Venus

Saturday - Saturn

No place for our planet earth, Uranus, and Neptune. In fact, earth is not taken for the planetary position in a person's horoscope as well, and the longitude and latitude of the place of birth are taken into account for the influence of other planets in a person's horoscope.

Planets have their influence in human lives

Coming Events Cast Their Shadow Before Them

Future events are revealed beforehand by God. He knows the past, the present, and the future. So, He wants to point out certain events likely to happen in the future beforehand. We can cite famous examples. When Jesus Christ was born, a bright star, the Star of Bethlehem, appeared in the sky, a good omen. Before Julius Caesar was assassinated, there was blood rain in the capital city, a ghost walked on the streets of Rome, and an owl was seen sitting in the marketplace during the day, which are bad omens. In our daily walk of life, we see good omens show up if there is a likelihood of success, and bad omens take place if there is a likelihood of failure while performing a specific task or proceeding on a journey to perform an important event. So, God is always with us, guiding us all along.

Light

Imagine the world in the absence of light. It is a nightmare. We cannot see anything. We cannot see one another. So, God created light and also created eyes. Was light created earlier? Or were the eyes created earlier? Perhaps not all living things need eyes. Some can survive without eyes. Plants have no eyes. They rely on the sense of touch only for their survival. The absence of eyes does not deter them from synthesising food by photosynthesis. But, in higher living organisms, the absence of eyes is a big handicap. We cannot determine how eyes have evolved. But, if there is no light, there will be no need for eyes! For argument's sake, the eyes might have evolved. But there is no proof as to the evolution of light! It should have been created. Apart from the sun, stars are a source of light. Candles and fire are also sources of light. They burn using oxygen in the atmosphere. Artificial lights can be lit using electricity. Light includes gamma rays, X rays, microwaves, and radio waves.

Light is electromagnetic radiation, the primary tool for perceiving the world. The main source of light energy for the Earth is the Sun. We have already discussed the pivotal role of the sun for the survival of living things on earth. The sun sustains the process of photosynthesis. Actually, the white light of the Sun consists of seven colours. Red, blue, and green are the primary colours. Orange, yellow, indigo, and violet are combinations of colours. Light travels in a straight line. It travels at a speed of 300,000 km per second. Without darkness, it is difficult to see the value and glory of light.

Light and Evolution of the Eye

Light is electromagnetic radiation that can be perceived by the human eye. Sources of light are many. The main source of light is the Sun. Artificial light can be created by electricity.

Eyes are exquisitely complicated organs. They act like cameras to collect and focus light and convert it into an electric signal that the brain translates into images.

Have the eyes evolved or been created by God? Why don't the plants have no eyes? Why didn't eyes evolve in plants? If the Sun is not present, what is the position regarding the evolution of eyes? A definite answer cannot be given. Eyes and Sun are creations of God.

Humans have camera-style eyes. However, compound eyes are more advanced than camera-style eyes. In large animals, camera-style eyes are present. Compound eyes are present in insects. They possess a very large angle and have the ability to detect fast movement. That is why it is difficult to hit a housefly. If compound eyes are more beneficial and advanced than camera-style eyes, why didn't they evolve in humans and other animals? In fact, there has always been a dire need for eyes on the rear side, so that rear view is beneficial. But why didn't human eyes evolve on the rear side, or did a compound eye not evolve to have a better perception?

Sound

Sound is another magnificent creation of God. Without sound, there will be no communication, no speech, and no languages. Had sound evolved over a period of time? The ears are the organs to hear the sound. Which originated first? Sound or ears? Ears are the organs created by God!

The source of sound vibrates, bumping into nearby air molecules, causing a mechanical disturbance from a state of equilibrium. Sound travels at a speed of 331 metres per second. Sound is a pressure wave, whereas light is a fundamental particle. Sound is a longitudinal wave, whereas light is a transverse wave. Sound is a mechanical wave, whereas light is an electromagnetic wave. Sound waves require a medium to travel, while light waves do not require a medium to travel. The vestibular system in the ears is responsible for balancing as well. Without air, sound has no value.

Medicinal Herbs

Of course, allopathic treatment cures almost all diseases in mankind. Diseases in mankind are numerous compared with other animals. For example, high blood pressure is not common in animals and birds. Because they seldom suffer from mental stress. It is the complicated mental condition that makes mankind vulnerable to diseases. Plants need water and nutrients in the soil. The basic need of animals and birds is food. There is no need for clothes for them at all. They spend almost their entire time in foraging. They live a happy life. They never bother about tomorrow. They live happily and die a natural death. Have we heard of any monkeys who were admitted to the intensive care unit in their old age? They rely on their own strength till their last breath. But, due to the complicated lifestyle created by mankind themselves, they are subjected to mental stress and agony. The basic needs of mankind are food and clothes. In fact, early mankind needed no dress at all, and like all animals, they only needed food, which they collected by foraging. But the dawn of civilisation was instrumental in the requirement of clothes. But mankind could not stop with food and clothes. They require the things they do not possess. Farmers who cultivated barley required wheat. So, they exchanged barley for wheat. This resulted in the barter system. And the life of mankind had become topsy-turvy with the invention of money. They have to run after money. Everything has a price. Nothing is available free of cost. We will discuss the effect of money in a later chapter. Allopathic treatment of diseases had developed only a century or two ago. Before that, mankind had to depend on herbs to cure their ailments. God has provided alkaloids and substances that can treat mankind's diseases. How do plants contain alkaloids? It is available in the earth. So, God has predesigned the life structure. God knows which diseases are likely to affect mankind and created herbals in anticipation. We will discuss some of the medicinal plants and herbs.

Garlic (cloves)

It possesses antimicrobial, cardioprotective, anticancer, and anti-inflammatory properties, and it lowers cholesterol and blood pressure.

As discussed earlier, none of the animals like eating garlic because of its pungent taste. In fact, animals do not need garlic because they are seldom affected by hypertension and cardiac diseases. But garlic is God's gift to mankind. Only mankind suffers from blood pressure and cardiac diseases, and garlic prevents the onset of these diseases.

Ginger (Root)

Anti-inflammatory and antioxidative properties.

Gingko(Leaf)

Asthma, Bronchitis, fatigue, and dementia

Goldenseal (root, rhizome)

Diahorrea, eye and skin irritations, antiseptic

Milk thistle (fruit)

Liver diseases and cancer

Saw palmetto (fruit)

Benign prostatic hyperplasia

Valerian (root)

Reduces sleeplessness and anxiety.

Chamomile (flower)

Anxiety and wound healing.

Echinacea(leaf, stalk and root)

Cold, flu

Feverfew (Leaf)

Fever, migraines, arthritis

Gale of the wind (Phyllanthus niruri)

Jaundice

Aloe Vera

Stomach ailments, laxative, anti-inflammatory, eczema, psoriasis and ulcers

Angelica

Digestive tonic and relieves poor appetite, dyspepsia and nausea

Arnica

Anti-inflammatory analgesic

Artemisia

Worm infestations, nerve tonic, fever and menstrual complaints

Basil

Natural disinfectant

Bergamot

Flatulence relieves cold and fever

Bilberry

Antioxidant properties which lower blood sugar and improve blood supply

Borage

Anti-inflammatory, dry and itching skin

Brahmi

Improves memory

Calendula

Anti-inflammatory, antimicrobial

Caraway

Bloating and flatulence

Catnip

Antispasmodic

Celery

Diuretic

Cinnamon

Protection against infection, improving circulation and digestion

Cloves

Antibacterial, mouthwash, anaesthetic

Coriander

Antispasmodic

Cumin

Indigestion, diarrhoea, stimulate the appetite

Dandelion

Therapeutic effects on kidneys and liver promote bile secretion and laxatives.

Echinacea

Stimulant for the immune system, detoxifying

Evening prime rose

Rheumatoid, arthritis, diabetic neuropathy and dermatitis

Eyebright

Remedy for irritated or inflamed conditions of the eye, conjunctivitis, catarrhal conditions, and middle ear infection.

Fenugreek

Cervical and liver cancer, oral contraceptive, aphrodisiac effects

Feverfew

Migraine headaches

Flax

Laxative

Garlic and onion

Antibiotic, bronchial infection, gastrointestinal infections.

Germander

Diseases of the brain

Ginger

Nausea, indigestion

Gotu Kola

Improves memory and longevity

Hops

Insomnia

Horsetail

Urinary tract problem

Juniper

Diuretic, antiseptic and antiviral

Lemon balm

Anxiety and depression

Lemongrass

Digestive upsets, stomach ache

Mustard

Antibacterial, antifungal

Parsley

Urinary tract disorders gout

Pine

Antiseptic, stimulant

Plantain

Inflammation, ulcers

Pomegranate

Antioxidant and anti-inflammatory

Red clover

Eczema and psoriasis in children

Rosemary

Tonic stimulant for nerves

Saffron

Blood and heart diseases and cancer

Sweet violet

Cancer

Tansy

Worm infestations

Green tea

Prevents cardiovascular diseases

Turmeric

Blood purifier, anti-cancer, protects the liver

Valerian

Aiding sleep

Viburnum

Muscular tension

Walnut

Heart attack and stroke

Solanum trilobatum

Asthma, cold and fever.

False Daisy. Eclipta prostatic

Liver diseases, anaemia, cold and jaundice.

Green chiretta, Andrographis paniculate (leaf and stem)

Dengue fever, prevention of covid 19

Chaste tree (leaves)

Mosquito repellent, treatment of cold and headache.

Scutch grass, Cynodondoctylon

Juice treats heat and ulcers. Purify blood and improve eyesight.

Withaniasomnifera (roots)

Reduces anxiety and sleeplessness. Helps in increasing the quality and quantity of semen.

Java plum, Syzygium cumin (seeds, fruits)

Diabetes, antioxidant

It contains calcium, Vitamin B1, B2 and B5. It helps purify the arteries, reducing the risk of heart attack and stroke.

The list is only illustrative and not exhaustive.

Allopathic Treatment and Medicines

Allopathy provides the most efficient treatment for diseases. Treatment with herbals is prolonged, whereas allopathy provides treatment for almost every disease of mankind. Doctors use medicines for treatment, which are chemicals or combinations of chemicals. It is needless to say, God has provided these chemicals for the preparation of medicines.

We may discuss some of the medicines and their properties:

Ether, Holothane: Anaesthesia.

Major surgeries cannot be performed while the patient is conscious, so the application of anaesthesia assumes significance. God knows it and provided medicines.

Diclofenac, Ibuprofen, Paracetamol: Antipyretics.

Cetirizine: Anaphylaxis.

Albendazole: Antihelminthics.

Amoxicillin, Ampicillin: Antibacterial.

Dapsone: Antileprosy.

Ethambutol, Ofloxacin: Antifungal.

Acyclovir: Antiviral.

Chloroquine phosphate, Quinine sulphate: Antimalarial.

Actinomycin, Cisplatin: Cytotoxic.

Cyanocobalamin, Iron dextran: Antianaemia.

Acetyl Salicylic acid: Antianginal.

Amlodipine: Antihypertensive.

Digoxin, Dobutamine: Heart failure.

Lignocaine: Ophthalmic.

Benzoin: Antiseptic.

Ranitidine: Gastrointestinal.

Zinc sulphate: Antidiarrheal.
Insulin: Diabetes.

Glucagon: Hyperglycaemia.

Salbutamol sulphate: Antiasthmatic.

The list is illustrative and not exhaustive, and it does not mean the medicines not mentioned are not effective. Many new medicines are continuously discovered, and the purpose of the book is not to provide a complete list of medicines. The purpose is to establish the fact that chemicals are already provided by God, and the only work of scientists is to discover them using the knowledge provided by God.

Money

God does not want mankind to live an ordinary life like other living beings. It is His desire to create differences among mankind, making some fortunate while making others less fortunate. So, He created, nay, made man create money and wealth.

Before the advent of money, the barter system was used. There was no problem for mankind when they were wanderers. Their only need was, like all animals, food, which they gathered without much difficulty. They needed no clothes at all! The dawn of civilisation resulted in an increased need for things other than food. Cultivators of barley needed wheat. They exchanged barley for wheat. But in due course of time, adopting the barter system became difficult. Cultivators of barley and wheat needed beef. But the producer of beef did not require the quantity of wheat and barley in exchange for beef. There was difficulty in reselling the surplus wheat and barley to others who were in requirement of the grains. After large-scale commercialisation, it was very difficult to adopt the barter system. So, a common exchange mechanism had to be devised. This resulted in the invention of money. Initially, various commodities had been used as money:

Wampum (beads made from shells): American Indians.

Cowries (brightly coloured shells): Indians.

Whale's teeth: Fijians.

Tobacco: North America.

Cigarettes: Post World War 2 in Germany.

Cattle: In primitive times.

These commodities were considered scarce in those times and were a medium of exchange. But later on, coins made of copper and silver were minted as a medium of common exchange. Later, after large-scale production of gold, gold coins were minted and used as a medium of exchange. As economies grew larger, the pace of production of these precious metals could not cope with the expansion of the economy. China was the first country to print paper currency thousand years ago. In the 18th and 19th centuries, paper money spread over the world.

Money is a medium of economic exchange. It is the medium in which prices and values are expressed and the principal measure of wealth. The basic function of money is to permit trade to take place without the double coincidence of barter. If a person has something to sell and wants something else in return, money is used to facilitate the desired exchange of items.

People of a country use the paper currency of that country. The issuance of currencies is bound by certain rules. A country cannot print and issue currency at will; reserves of precious metals have to be kept for the quantity of notes printed. In the present global scenario, no country can be self-reliant. Every country cannot produce the exact requirements of its people. For instance, Gulf countries do not produce sufficient agricultural produce for the requirements of their people; they have to import food items. At the same time, they produce oil, which is many times the requirement of their people. They tend to export oil to countries that are deficient in oil production. So, export and import are mandatory for every country. If the quantum of exports is higher, the balance of payment position is favourable to that country. If imports are more than exports, the balance of payment is unfavourable to that country. A rise in a particular country's quantity of money would tend to raise prices in that country relative to prices in other countries. The rise in prices would consequently discourage exports and encourage imports. The decreased supply of foreign currency, due to a decrease in exports and the increased demand for foreign currency to pay for imports, would tend to raise the price of foreign currency in comparison with domestic currency. This is exactly what is happening in countries such as Sri Lanka. The other side of the coin is China, where almost the production of most commodities exceeds the requirement of that country. Exports are greater than imports, and the balance of payment position is favourable to China vis-a-vis the superpower, the USA.

The dollar, the currency of the USA, is used in many other countries as a medium of exchange. It is said that two-thirds of all dollars in circulation are outside the USA. The role of paper currency is decreasing due to Electronic Money Transfer. Money is transferred without the actual physical transfer of paper currency.

Money and material possessions act as a check on the population explosion. In a family, if more children are born, the resources have to be distributed among the children, resulting in lower distribution. So families plan to have only one or two children. Still, the population of the world reached 8 billion. If the resources were vast, the population might have increased manifold.

Money and human life are inseparable. For every pursuit, every human needs money. In fact, money is responsible for the disparities among mankind, separating them into upper, upper-middle, lower-middle, poor, and ultra-poor. How a person utilises their skills, talents, ability, and intelligence to earn money is important. Each and every human has a unique talent; whether that talent helps in earning money or not, it is of no use if they possess skills and talents, but they are of no use in earning money. Thinking of money and earning it are altogether different.

Money is so central to our lives that, rich or poor, both should have a relationship with money. Money provides humans with security and stability besides offering a means to take care of families. Money is the cause of happiness as well as stress. There is no upper ceiling for the possession of money, and humans never derive satisfaction from having sufficient money. If such satisfaction were to occur, there would be stagnation, and aspirations for wealth would cease, which could be detrimental to economic growth. If you were to ask any human, "Do you have sufficient money?" Certainly, "No" would be the answer. Money is to be used consciously, wisely, and with enjoyment. It should be approached with a sense of optimism, clarity, and openness instead of dread.

Invention of currency notes by the Chinese is a revelation

Salt

Salt is an essential nutrient containing sodium and chloride. As we know, salt is available only in seawater. It is needless to emphasise that this is an arrangement by God. Salt has accumulated in the sea primarily from runoff water from the land, rivers, and openings in the seafloor over a period of many epochs. Salt is available in seawater in the proportion of 35 parts per thousand. Salt is produced from seawater by evaporation. During evaporation, seawater evaporates, and the salt remains as a residue. The quantity of salt available in seawater is so large that if all the salt in the ocean is removed and spread evenly on the earth's surface, it would form a layer of more than 500 feet. The approximate weight of salt in seawater is 120 million tonnes. Salt adds to the taste of food. Without salt, food will not be delicious. Salt plays a crucial role in human health. Salt is the main source of sodium and chloride ions. Sodium is important for nerve and muscle function, maintaining blood pressure, and maintaining fluid levels.

At one point in time, salt was a scarce commodity and paid as wages to labourers. The word 'salary' had its roots in the word 'salt.' Salt is considered a divine substance and described as dear to God, and importance is attached to it in religious ceremonies. Salt is often associated with fertility. Without both water and salt, cells could not get nourishment and would die of dehydration.

Salt is a chemical term for a substance produced by the reaction of an acid with a base. Sodium, an unstable metal that can suddenly burst into flame, reacts with a deadly poisonous gas known as chlorine, becoming sodium chloride NaCl. Chloride is essential for digestion and respiration. Without sodium, which the body cannot manufacture, the body would be unable to transport nutrients or oxygen, transmit nerve impulses, or move muscles, including the heart muscles. An adult human being contains about 250 grams of salt but is constantly losing it through bodily functions. It is essential to replace this lost salt. Egyptians used salt to make mummies, and salt is associated with longevity and permanence.

Bringing bread and salt to a new home is a Jewish tradition dating back to the Middle Ages. In Indian culture, salt is bought on auspicious days as it is considered a symbol of wealth. In both Islam and Judaism, salt seals a bargain because it is immutable. Ancient Egyptians, Greeks, and Romans included salt in sacrifices and offerings. In Christianity, salt is associated not only with longevity and permanence but, by extension, with truth and wisdom. The Catholic Church dispenses not only holy water but also holy salt.

Humans need a maximum of 16 pounds a year based on the level of sweating and physical work. Physical labourers need more salt because they must replace the salt that is lost in sweating. Salt deficiency causes headaches, weakness, and nausea. If deprived for long, the victim will die. A horse requires five times the salt intake of a human, and a cow needs ten times the amount of salt a human requires.

Until the production of salt started in large quantities, it was a scarce commodity. Salt represented wealth. The Chinese, the Romans, and the French taxed it to raise money for wars. It was used in lieu of money. The Chinese were the first to produce salt. In the 2nd century BC, Yi Dun rose to prominence by producing salt in pans, by boiling brine in the pan, one of the leading techniques for the next 2000 years. As salt was expensive, sprinkling salt directly on food had been a rarity.

The history of the USA is one of constant warfare over salt. Whoever controlled salt was in power. This was true before Europeans arrived and it continued to be the reality until after the American Civil War.

Sugar

The presence of sugar in sugarcane and sugar beet is not coincidental but an arrangement by God. Sugarcane contains 10 to 18 percent of sugar by weight, while sugar beet contains up to 22 percent by weight. Sugar is a carbohydrate. The chemical formula of sugar (sucrose) is $C_{12}H_{22}O_{11}$. Glucose, fructose, and galactose are monosaccharides. Sucrose, lactose, and maltose are disaccharides. Sucrose is a combination of glucose and fructose. Lactose is a combination of glucose and galactose. Maltose is a combination of glucose and glucose. In fruits, fructose is present, whereas in milk, lactose is present. Starch is a sugar found in plants and is a source of abundant energy in human food. However, overconsumption of sugar may lead to obesity, diabetes, cardiovascular diseases, and tooth decay. Sugar is God-made, but these diseases are manmade.

There are six tastes required for human health, and our diet should contain all the six tastes.

Taste	Present in	Functions in the body
Sweet	Sugarcane, Sugarbeet	Builds tissues
Salty	Sea water	Cleanses tissues
Sour	Tamarind, citrus	Improves taste to food, lubricates tissues, stimulates digestion etc,
Pungent	Chilli, pepper	Stimulates digestion and metabolic activities
Bitter	Bitter gourd	Detoxifies and lighten tissues
Astringent	Unripe banana, legumes	Absorbs water and dries fats

God has provided all six tastes required for maintaining our health. Sources of five tastes, except salt, are plants. Salt is available in seawater. Excess or deficient consumption of any of the six tastes may lead to health complications.

Advent of Science and Technology and Increase in Employment

As long as humankind remained wanderers, there was no dearth; in fact, there was no need for employment. But the dawn of civilisation resulted in multiple requirements. The multiple requirements combined with the ever-increasing population demanded additional avenues of jobs. Until the invention of electricity, most jobs were in the fields of agriculture, masonry, and hand weaving. The discovery of electricity created additional avenues of employment. Most countries in the world became industrialised. Industrialisation resulted in umpteen employment opportunities. Industries began to blossom in the fields of textiles, steel, vehicle production, etc.

A revelation happened in the 20th century with the invention of computers. Anyone in the year 1970 or 1980 could not have expected such a large potential for computer and Information technology and the large-scale employment the industry provided to millions of people. Millions of jobs have been created in software and hardware. God has been creating additional avenues of jobs for the ever-increasing population.

Innumerable Diseases of Mankind

Of course, various diseases affect every living thing. Viruses and bacteria affect and cause diseases. But humans are affected by innumerable diseases. Animals suffer from fewer diseases than mankind. Animals need nothing except food and shelter. But the requirements of humans are more complex. Humans cannot satisfy themselves only with food and shelter. The activity of the brain is highly complex in humans. The cause for anxiety is restricted to survival in animals and birds, but the cause for anxiety is numerous in mankind. Diabetes and blood pressure seldom affect animals and birds. They seldom overeat and do not live a sedentary lifestyle. But there was no problem for humans as long as they lived a wandering life. But the dawn of civilisation spoiled the good life of humans.

Diseases affecting humans are innumerable. And in turn, various branches have evolved in the medical treatment of humans. Cardiology, Orthopaedics, Nephrology, Oncology, Neurology, Ophthalmology, Gastroenterology, ENT, Gynaecology, Rheumatology, Endocrinology are the specialised branches. Has anyone heard of an animal affected by ischaemic stroke? Or affected by Parkinson's disease? Almost all of them live happily until the end of their life sustaining themselves, seldom needing anybody's support.

Mosquitoes

Mosquitoes are said to have evolved from grasshoppers, in which mouthparts are in a more primitive condition. But any living being is part of the food chain. Mosquitoes are harmful and make a nuisance to humans and animals, but they play a substantial role in the ecosystem. Mosquitoes form an important source of biomass in the food chain, serving as food for fish as larvae and for birds, bats, and frogs as adult flies. Some species of mosquitoes are important pollinators. For example, grasshoppers cannot serve as food to these living beings, and hence God has evolved mosquitoes.

Female mosquitoes need a blood meal to produce eggs, hence they require biting humans and animals. Male mosquitoes only drink sugary fluids and have less specialised mouthparts. In female mosquitoes, the antenna smells the host, and a bundle of six stylets forms a tube that pierces the skin. Mosquitoes need only one thousandth of the effort we make to pierce the skin with a needle. Is it by evolution?

Lifespan of a Species

The lifespan of most species is not infinite. Lifespans vary from 1-10 million years. Almost 99.9% of all species that live on Earth have become extinct. Will mankind also go extinct?

Lifespan is the period between birth and death of an organism. Lifespan vastly varies among organisms. The lifespan of humans varies from country to country. Japanese people have a longer lifespan. Why is life not eternal? How do cells age? Some perennial trees live for about 200 years. Trees that are 4000 years old are said to be surviving on Earth.

Seasonal crops have a lifespan of 90-120 days. Imagine, wheat is a perennial crop! It may grow 100 feet tall. Not only is harvesting difficult, but also the yield will be affected. Almost all the lifespans of seasonal crops are short, but in animals, lifespan varies. If the conditions are favourable, wheat and barley, etc., mature within 120 days. Almost all cereals and pulses meant for human consumption have short lifespans. Is it a result of evolution? No cereal or pulse is perennial. How has grass evolved? Grasses fulfil the fodder requirement of hares, goats, and cattle. Grasses play an important role in the food chain. So, the evolution of grasses is purposeful and not spontaneous.

However, in humans, lifespan largely varies. A week-old baby may likely die; death may come at 10, 20, 30, 40, or 50 years. Not all humans are able to live for 80 or 90 years. Innumerable diseases affect mankind. Heredity and food habits mainly determine longevity. In countries such as Japan, longevity is higher compared to countries such as Somalia and Ethiopia, which are poverty-stricken, and medical facilities are poor.

Greenland sharks and Bowhead whales live for about 150 years. Giant tortoises live for 190 years. Ocean Quahog and Red sea urchins live for 200 years. Immortal jellyfish live eternally unless they are killed by accident.

Rate of Respiration and Longevity

Species with a slow rate of respiration have longer longevity. In humans, the rate of respiration varies among individuals, as does longevity. On average, humans breathe 12-18 times per minute. Air should be inhaled for 4 seconds, held for 7 seconds, and then slowly exhaled. A decrease in the rate of respiration will result in an increase in longevity and vice versa. Tortoises have a very slow rate of respiration and have high longevity.

Why Hadn't Only Good Virtues Evolved in mankind?

People certainly know what is good and what is bad. Many preachers taught mankind to follow good virtues and shun bad things detrimental to mankind. If only good thoughts developed in mankind, it should be free from any sin. But people can be divided into various categories. Some have good thoughts only and do only good to mankind. But this category is very minimal. Some have more good thoughts than bad thoughts. The majority of people fall into this category. Some have more bad thoughts than good thoughts. Some others have only bad thoughts and do only bad deeds. This category is also very minimal.

It is God's design for humans to exist in various categories. Otherwise, only good humans might have evolved due to evolution.

Ageing and Death

Ageing results from the impact of the accumulation of a wide variety of molecular and cellular damage over a period of time. This leads to a gradual decrease in physical and mental capacity. The risk of diseases increases with age and results in death. Old age is characterised by the onset of geriatric syndrome, hearing loss, cataracts, osteoarthritis, pulmonary diseases, depression, and dementia.

Ageing can be defined as the time-related deterioration of the physiological functions necessary for survival and fertility. A cell can be replicated about 50 times, and after that, genetic material is no longer able to be copied. The cell will lose its functional characteristics. The accumulation of senescent cells is cellular ageing. With ageing, the secretion of hormones will begin to diminish, leading to changes in the skin and bone density. Ageing slows down the metabolic process. The capacity of cells to turn food into energy decreases with age.

Why can evolution not provide a clue to prevent ageing? If the theory of evolution is to be believed, living things tend to improve continually. If so, why do human cells cannot be replicated more than 50 times? And thereby, why can mankind not live for 10000 years? Or live eternally like immortal jellyfish? As per the theory of evolution, desired changes occur in an organism over a period of time. Any living organism likes to live eternally, let alone, a long life. But, living organisms cannot prevent ageing and, ultimately, death. Nature plays a role in this. What is nature? Of course, it is God.

Death ultimately happens to any living being. Why has evolution not provided immortality to living beings? Despite mankind's discoveries and inventions, mankind cannot conquer death. Why?

There will be a scramble for food and space if all living beings attain immortality. So, it is God's wish that all living beings should die.

We know what happens to the body after death. But body and soul are interdependent. If the soul departs from the body, the body becomes meaningless and begins to decay. So, the soul needs a body, and the body needs a soul. But what happens to the soul when the soul departs from the body? Soul also die? Or it goes to heaven or hell? Where are heaven and hell? How does the soul travel to heaven or hell?

Cement

Cement is a binding material used for construction. No doubt, God has provided raw materials for manufacturing cement. Cement is only behind water as the most consumed substance on earth. Cement is mixed with sand to bind together. Initially, lime and volcanic ash were used for construction. Cement is a mixture of calcium oxide and silicon dioxide. Cement is produced from limestones. Cement, when reinforced with steel, makes Reinforced Cement Concrete rock hard and is used for the construction of dams and skyrocketing buildings. The prevalence of raw materials for the production of cement is not spontaneous, but God has provided the raw materials on earth and provided humans with the knowledge to discover the method of production for large-scale use.

Vegetable Oil

Vegetable oils are used for cooking, and certain oils like castor oil have industrial uses, too. The presence of oil in certain seeds seems to be God's arrangement. The presence of oil in seeds is of no use in seed germination. Oil is obtained from palm, soybean, rapeseed, sunflower, groundnut, sesame, mustard, coconut, olive, rice bran, etc. Some oils are extremely beneficial to mankind. For example, sesame oil has low fat and is good for the heart.

Commercialisation

Except for man, no living organism needs wealth. The greed for amassing wealth made all other living organisms subservient to mankind. No upper ceiling can be fixed for wealth. Commercialisation resulted in inequality among mankind. At the same time, the rich bathe in millions; a square meal a day is not available to the less privileged. Here, destiny plays its role. Those people whose ancestors were kind-hearted and helpful to other living organisms are now affluent, and those whose ancestors sinned have to suffer. Destiny can be altered to a certain extent by benevolence during the lifetime of a man.

The greed of mankind resulted in the domestication of animals for the economic betterment of mankind. A great example is oxen. Before the invention of tractors, oxen were used to plough the field and draw water from wells to irrigate the field. Cows were domesticated for milk. Of course, the milk is meant for their calves, but mankind successfully stole milk, denying the calves their share. How oxen and cows evolved cannot be deciphered, but their utility to mankind is humongous. Their evolution reveals the fact that God has designed evolution for the ultimate utility of mankind. Why could mankind not tame an elephant to plough the field? The evolution of every creature is specifically designed by God. Dogs were domesticated for hunting and for providing safety to houses from thieves and other unwarranted trespassers. Goats and chicken have evolved for meat requirements. They are grown on a large scale for commercial purposes. Normally, a chick is fully grown in 6 months, and humans have successfully modified their genes, and the chick becomes fully grown in 6 weeks! Country chickens normally lay 100 eggs a year. But their genes have been modified, and they were made to lay eggs every day, and at the end of their egg-laying capacity, they were hulled for meat! All these poor creatures lost their independence and made scapegoats of commercialisation.

Rivers

Seawater cannot be used for agriculture and drinking purposes even though there is no dearth of seawater on earth. Humans need fresh water. Rivers are God-made arrangements to fulfil the needs of living beings. Rivers are natural streams of water that flow in a channel with banks on both sides. A river is a naturally flowing watercourse and flows from the surface at a higher altitude to the sea, which is at a lower altitude. The landscape is so beautifully designed by God that the structure of earth is adapted for the origin of rivers at high altitudes, particularly in dense forests, where the soil and the trees can suck the rainwater and release the water gradually to form streams and, ultimately, rivers. Rivers are also formed by the gradual melting of glaciers. Glaciers are able to replenish rivers so that they remain perennial. 97% of the water of the earth is present in oceans. In rivers, only 0.025 % of water is present. Rivers are nourished by precipitation, overland runoff, and the melting of ice at the edge of snowfields and glaciers. Rivers are ancient settlement sites for humans. Amazon is the world's principal river.1/5th water in all Rivers in the world runs through the Amazon. It originates in the Andes mountains of Peru in South America. The world's largest tropical rainforest is in the Amazon. The Nile, Yangtze, and Mississippi are principal rivers. Barring a few, all countries have rivers.

A river flows downhill as a small stream. Precipitation and groundwater add to the river flow. A river is also fed by its tributaries. Amazon has 1000 tributaries. The movement of water in a river is called current. As the river enters steeper slopes, the river receives more energy. Hydroelectric generation is made in the river system using the flow of water. Fertile soil along rivers is good for cultivating crops. Some of the world's most important river systems are given below.

Amazon - South America

The Nile - Egypt, Africa

Indus - South Asia

Tigris and Euphrates. Middle East

Huang - China

Volga - Europe

Thames - England

Rhine - Europe

Yangtze - Asia

Ganges - Indian subcontinent

Mississippi, Colorado - North America

Congo - Africa

Excess water in rivers during the rainy season flows into the sea. It is a very important phenomenon to sustain the level of salt in the ocean. If the flow of the river water into the sea is altogether stopped, the content of salt in the seawater will increase, and the water level in the sea will decrease, although by a small percentage, thereby resulting in the increase of saltiness in the seawater which is detrimental to the lands adjacent to seashore.

Early human civilisations flourished on river banks

Electric Vehicles

Though electricity has been discovered centuries earlier, electric vehicles are gaining importance only now. Petroleum is the main fuel used by vehicles. How plants and trees submerged millions of years ago have been converted into petroleum remains an interesting mystery. We have every reason to believe that it is an act of God.

Capillary Force, Centrifugal Force, and Centripetal Force

Capillary force

Capillary force is a force that defies gravitational force. Capillary action is the process of a liquid flowing in a narrow space, defying gravity. This occurs due to adhesive and cohesive forces. Capillary action causes the upward movement of groundwater through the different zones of soil. Water is transported inside the xylem of plants' vessels by capillary action. So, capillary action plays a vital role in sending water upwards. Without capillary force, plants cannot sustain themselves. It is interesting to know that while gravitation is responsible for every act on earth, there remains a force that is opposite to gravitation. It is an act of God.

Centripetal force

Centripetal force is a force that acts on a body moving in a circular path and is directed toward the centre of the circular path. Centripetal force always points towards the centre of the circle. Hence, the direction of the moving body is constantly changing.

Centrifugal force

A force that is exerted on an object moving in a curved path that acts outwardly away from the centre of rotation. Centrifugal force is a fictitious force the object experiences during circular motion. It is interesting to know that centripetal and centrifugal forces are opposite in nature, but both forces are experienced by rotating objects simultaneously. It is an act of God.

Are these forces due to the rotation and revolution of the earth? Nothing substantial has been established so far, but relativity cannot be ruled out.

Deities and Devils

God bestows benevolence. God is omnipotent and omnipresent. Gods live in heaven.

Devils are destructive and malevolent. They harm and are evil. It is ironic that God and the Devil exist side by side. It is God's wish to keep the devils side by side. Otherwise, He might have wiped them off.

The Sweet Taste of Fruits. Is it by Evolution?

The content of sugar increases with the ripening of fruits. Fructose, a sugar that is present in fruits, increases with the ripening. The sweet taste of fruits evolved? Or a God-made arrangement for the benefit of a living being? Because of their sweet taste, fruits are beneficial to birds and animals. The sweet taste also helps with their better seed dispersal.

Dispersal of Seeds

It is difficult to believe the seed dispersal mechanism had evolved over a period of time. The seeds of Dandelion and Calotropis are attached to a lightweight, silky fibre, which is flown away by the wind to different places. Winged seeds are present in Maple trees. When the seeds fall from a tree, they do not fall just below the tree, but the wings rotate as the seed falls from the tree, thereby assisting the seed to travel farther away from the tree. The seeds of mangrove trees are dispersed by water. Dispersal through animals and birds is present in some plants. For example, birds eat neem fruits, and the bird's digestive system helps to weaken the tough coat around seeds so that germination is easy. Some seeds disperse through the explosion. In peas and flax, the fruits explode, and the seeds are thrown away in different places. Have these plants evolved the seed dispersal mechanism? If so, what were the previous seed dispersal mechanism? Why did in coconut, seed dispersal mechanism fail to evolve?

Destiny, Balancing of Work and Role of God

Why are there so many variations in people's destiny? Some are born rich and continue to be rich. Some are born in abject poverty and continue to toil in poverty throughout their life. Some are born poor but are able to progress and become rich. Some others are born rich and indulge in extravagance, becoming poor. In fact, the earth's resources are for all. Why is there much inequality in attaining the resources? Even three square meals a day are not available to many people, while some others attain all the wealth they require and even more than what they require. In fact, it is God's wish for the inequalities among mankind to exist. Mankind may go unruly and may not be afraid to commit sins if all are equal. So, God wants to create a moral fear among mankind before committing any sin. But, still, mankind has the temerity to commit sins without fear, fully knowing the consequences. This is the reason why these inequalities exist. There are no inequalities among elephants or deers in attaining the food they require. If humans remained as wanderers, they also needed nothing more than food. And additionally, clothes might have been required. At first, their requirement is limited to food. Then came the requirement of clothes. Their needs kept on increasing. And it culminated in the invention of money. And inequalities began to increase dramatically.

Why and how is the destiny of mankind shaped? Who shapes destiny? In fact, all are born equal on the earth, so why is there so much inequality? Can anyone explain the reasons? The body gets aged over a period of time and gets exterminated on death. But the soul never dies. God determines the destiny based on the good/bad deeds of ancestors. It can be revealed through horoscopes and palmistry. Expert astrologers can determine a person's destiny. Needless to say, efforts need to be put by the person in the direction of destiny shaped by God, and the person will achieve the position determined by destiny shaped by God. As mentioned earlier, destiny can be altered to a certain extent, though not as a whole, by good deeds.

Why Are Frogs Amphibians But Not Fish?

Frogs can live in water and land. But why fishes cannot live on land? Didn't fishes try to come to land? Only frogs tried to come to land and became successful? Does the theory of evolution provide any definite answer? Man is always trying to fly in the air. Why hadn't wings developed? Why can mankind not live in water? If mankind continues to make efforts to live in water for many generations, will a breathing mechanism evolve as in the case of frogs? Why didn't evolution could not provide enormous strength to mankind for their survival but provide them with abnormal mental powers instead? Why didn't such advanced mental powers develop in other species? God has made the humans supreme and not the evolution.

Herbivores and Carnivores – Balancing of Running Power

Carnivores rely on herbivores for food. Herbivores develop faster legs to outrun carnivores, but the legs of herbivores are not fast enough to outsmart them entirely. If the herbivores entirely outrun carnivores, then carnivores will be starved to death. On the other hand, if the carnivores outrun herbivores, then the herbivores will be wiped out from the earth. So, God maintains a balance between herbivores and carnivores and thereby ensures the existence of both.

Natural Enemies in the Animal Kingdom

Though innumerable examples can be cited for examples of natural enemies in the animal kingdom, familiar examples are snakes and mongooses and cats and rats. Why snakes and mongoose are natural enemies? Why bandicoots, which are similar in size to the mongoose and snake are, not natural enemies?

Carbohydrates, Plants, and Human Food

Amylopectin is a plant starch that is a major source of carbohydrates in most human diets. How did the human body evolve to derive energy from carbohydrates? The evolution of plants, the evolution of animals that depend on plants for food, and the provision of carbohydrates in plants, which is a source of energy for animals, are planned steps taken by God in evolution.

Why Can Xerophytic Plants Not Survive in Aquatic Habitats, and Vice Versa?

Species such as cactus are capable of enduring severe xerophytic conditions. Modified leaves and stems and the presence of cuticles curtail evaporation. Cactus cannot survive in aquatic conditions. As such, aquatic plants such as Vallisneria cannot survive in xerophytic conditions. Contrary to xerophytes, they have specialised structures to facilitate quick evaporation. Does this mean that xerophytes never tried to live in aquatic conditions? What prevented xerophytes from becoming accustomed to aquatic conditions and evolving into new species?

Why not other plants modify their structure to endure xerophytic conditions?

Camouflaging in Plants

How some plants evolved camouflaged mechanisms is a point to ponder. Have they evolved themselves, or has God bestowed them the power of camouflaging? Pebble plants have thick round leaves, coloured like stones and pebbles, to provide camouflage and protection against animals. Water hemlock, Birthwort, and Crowfoots are poisonous plants. If animals eat them, they will die. To attract male bees, the Bee orchid has a lip that looks and smells like a female bee. But, if no bees come along, the orchid can bend over to pollinate itself. Some lotus seeds have sprouted after being in a dormant state for 400 years. Sycamore seeds have wings to help them spin away in the wind. The Welwitschia plant, from the deserts of Southern Africa, can live up to 2000 years.

Camouflaging in Animals

Angel sharks have the same colour as the sand. They blend perfectly into the sandy seabed as they lie in wait for prey. With their long, thin bodies, stick insects look like leafless twigs. The ability of chameleons to change colour is a well-known example of camouflaging. Did the animals evolve the ability to camouflage? Or did God evolve them?

Garden lizard and chameleon are almost similar. However, chameleons are able to change colour, while garden lizards cannot. Did chameleons evolve from garden lizards, or did garden lizards evolve from chameleons? Protruding eyes for great field vision and sticky tongues to grab prey are common for garden lizards and chameleons. But garden lizards cannot change their colour as chameleons do. If chameleons evolved from garden lizards, did some garden lizards evolve into chameleons while some remained themselves as garden lizards? Similar is the case with mankind. If apes evolved into humans, why did some apes remain as apes? This is proof that evolution, even if it takes place, is shaped by God.

Why Did Snake and Eagle Choose to Be Non-vegetarian?

Why did snakes and eagles evolve as non-vegetarians? Why did they not prefer to eat grass instead? There is no dearth of grass. The food chain and food web have been beautifully designed by God.

Why are there no legs for a snake and multiple legs for a centipede?

To run fast, animals and reptiles need legs. In this aspect, snakes are in dire need of many legs, but why rapid movement by vertebrae evolved instead is a mystery. But, the irony is that centipedes, which are small and short compared to snakes, have hundreds of legs. Still, they move slower than snakes. Snakes have to move to catch the prey. But why legs have not evolved in snakes is a mystery.

Plumage in Peacocks and Parrots

Peacocks have beautifully designed feathers, and in peahens, feathers are absent. These beautiful feathers are supposedly evolved to attract peahen. Can we presume that initially, the beautiful feathers were absent, and the peacocks wished that they might be at an advantage if they had beautiful feathers, and as a result, the beautiful feathers gradually evolved? Can evolution cater to the desires of living beings.?

In Eclectus parrots, males and females have very different plumage. The male has bright green, while the female has red with a blue belly and a black bill. These contrasting colours have evolved spontaneously. Do the peacocks desire to have these colours?

Why haven't other birds developed beautiful plumage as in peacock?

The Big Pouch of Pelican

Pelicans collect fish in the pig pouch that hangs beneath their long necks. If evolution is responsible for the development of the big pouch, why such a big pouch has not evolved in other birds that feed on fish is an unanswered question.

Evolution of Bats

Bats are the only flying mammals. While other flying creatures, such as birds, lay eggs, how bats evolved to be mammals is an interesting question.

Different Reproductive Mechanisms in Amphibians and Mammals

Frogs, which are amphibians, lay hundreds of eggs, while mammals deliver a few or a single offspring. How have these different types of reproductive mechanisms evolved?

Why Sustainable Running Power Has Not Evolved in Cheetahs?

The cheetah is the fastest-running land animal, reaching 105 km/hour. It will run out of energy after a mere 30 seconds of sprinting. Why have cheetahs not evolved a sustainable running power? Had this power been developed in Cheetahs, no deer would have survived on Earth, and the deer might have been wiped out from Earth. Here is how the balancing power of God works! He wants both deer and cheetahs to survive, and so has not given sustainable running power to cheetahs. However, though slower runners compared with cheetahs, the hyenas have higher sustainable running capacity and are able to run consistently for long durations. They also prey on animals that get exhausted quickly.

Black and White Stripes of Zebras

How and why do black and white stripes evolve in zebras? Have the zebras chosen these colours? Why is the colour not yellow and green? While horses have no stripes, why do zebras have stripes? Every species should have its own identity, and so God evolves every species with a unique identity.

Stripes of Tiger

Tiger's stripes help to camouflage as it hides in tall grass and thick vegetation. Tigers cannot evolve these stripes on their own, but God evolved these stripes to suit the requirement.

Spongy Paw of a Cat

The bottom of a cat's paw has tufts of soft fur that help muffle the sound as it silently stalks its prey. Cats cannot evolve these spongy paws on their own, but God evolved them.

Archerfish

In a peculiar way of predating, Archerfish shoots down prey with water and devours the prey.

How the archer fish evolved the peculiar way of preying?

Why do whales come to the top of the water?

Whales can stay underwater, holding their breath for up to 2 hours at a time. But they have to inhale air. Why did an alternate respiring mechanism not evolve in whales, as in the case of fish that respire in the water through gills?

Comb Types in Chicken

Cocks have a comb, whereas in hen comb is rudimentary. Does this mean that cocks desired to have combs? And as a result, combs evolved? There are 9 types of combs: Single, rose, pea, walnut, cushion, strawberry, buttercup, V-shaped, and carnation. How and why combs evolved in cocks is an interesting question.

Sunflower

Angiosperms have flowers. Flowers are absent in thallophyta, bryophyta, pteridophyta and gymnosperms. Of course, plants depend on the sun for photosynthesis. But sunflower always faces the sun. Is it by evolution? Why didn't this character develop in other plants? Why haven't other plants evolved phototropism?

Sensitivity in Touch Me Not Plant

If we touch the Touch-me-not-plant, the leaves tend to droop. It is due to the decrease in turgid pressure. Is it by evolution? What prevented other plants from evolving this property?

Cotton

Has cotton been created by God to meet the requirement for cloth? Or did it evolve independently from other species? The soft, fluffy staple fibre that grows from the seed coat, the outer layer of the cotton plant's seeds, is separated from the seeds and used for making fabric. In fact, fluffy fibre is not very useful in the dispersal of seeds. Evolution cannot provide a definite answer. The quantity of fibre present in cotton does hinder the seed dispersal mechanism. In comparison, Calotropis has a better seed dispersal mechanism. The seeds in Calotropis are light in weight; fibre is much less in quantity. However, in cotton, the quantity of fibre is much higher, and the seeds have greater weight. This proves the fact that God has devised cotton for mankind's cloth requirement.

Computers

Man has discovered/invented many things for the benefit of mankind and thereby also assists other living beings. It has culminated in the invention of computers. A computer is a machine that can be programmed to carry out sequences of arithmetic or logical operations. It has the ability to store, retrieve and process data. The invention of the Integrated Circuit in 1958 is a revelation. The Central Processing Unit is the brain of the computer. The size of the computers has been unwieldy in the beginning. The size kept on decreasing. Nowadays, smartphones or tablets use a system on a chip. They were complete computers on a microchip, the size of the coin.

Humans may take credit for the invention of computers. But, without semiconductors, computers cannot function. Silicon and germanium, which are used in the production of semiconductors, are available on Earth. Batteries for electric vehicles are made from lithium, which is also available on Earth in its natural form. God has provided every metal and mineral required for future inventions. Can anyone explain where and how these metals and minerals came from? How the Big Bang resulted in the formation of planets containing various metals and minerals. Most of the metals and minerals are used for inventions by humans. So, these future inventions have been anticipated and predetermined by God. The presence of all kinds of metals and minerals on earth is surprising.

Artificial Intelligence and Robots

The invention of computers is a great boon to mankind. Vast data can be stored and retrieved within seconds. Artificial Intelligence, which can be compared to human Intelligence, is making a revolution. Robots can do manual work in hazardous industries. Mankind may invent computers and artificial intelligence but cannot create a single new species by modifying an existing species, though mankind may modify the characters of existing species, as in the case of broiler chicken.

How Does God Find Out the Good Deeds and Sins of Mankind?

How God watches the good and evil deeds of mankind? Mankind indulges in various activities. In mankind, some of them are kind-hearted, and some are ruthless. Some are a combination of both, depending on various external factors. In fact, among all the extant species of earth, Homo Sapiens is entirely different in having huge variations in behaviour and character.

The purpose of respiration is to inhale oxygen in the atmosphere to send to all parts of the body through the lungs and heart, as well as remove the carbon dioxide from the atmosphere. As we discussed in an earlier chapter, oxygen, which is a waste product in photosynthesis, is very vital for living organisms having aerobic respiration. Similarly, Carbon dioxide, which is a waste product in respiration, is very much required in food synthesis, in the form of carbon dioxide. We have reason to believe that God watches every activity of man through respiration, making respiration mandatory for higher living organisms.

Killing by a lion is not a sin, as killing is for food, which is essential for the survival of the lion. Animals seldom kill other animals except for food. But humans tend to harass fellow humans and other living organisms due to vengeance, hatred, jealousy, etc.; they also harass and kill animals for joy in the name of hunting! We, humans, may boast of inventing computers and, thereby, artificial intelligence, chat GPT, etc. But how precisely God finds out the good and evil deeds of mankind startles us. Does He have supercomputers more powerful than the ones we, mankind, have? He settles scores depending on the gravity of the crime committed. Likely, good deeds are also rewarded.

Unnecessary harassing or killing of fellow humans or living beings is a sin. We should not remove or kill even a plant unnecessarily. Felling of trees is a sin in some religions. We should help fellow humans and other living beings in whatever ways possible to us.

Extraordinary Capacity of Animals Compared to Man

If a cat's eye is hidden with a cloth and the cat is taken miles away from home, it has the capacity to return home. Almost mankind lacks this keen instinct. Similarly, the smelling capacity of dogs is extraordinary compared to mankind. Even tiny ants have extraordinary smelling power. If sugar is placed farther away from ants, they smell and reach within minutes. Ants are extraordinarily agile. They move at an extraordinary speed relative to their size. They are diligent and hard-working. They can lift weight which is many times higher than their own weight. Humans are no match for ants in these instincts. A bird is much smaller in size, and its level of intelligence is negligible compared to that of mankind. But can humans build a bird's nest? God has provided a higher level of keen instinct to birds in this regard. Spiders are tiny creatures compared to mankind. Spinnert glands located in the abdomen of the spiders secrete proteinaceous spider silk used for making the web. All the edges of the web are almost exactly located at the same distance from the centre of the web. How a spider judges the distance of the web is a mystery unresolved. The theory of evolution has no answer for the absence of these keen instincts in mankind. Though there is a dire need for these keen instincts in mankind, the absence of these keen instincts proves that God has devised separate evolutionary mechanisms for every organism. Why could mankind not develop these keen instincts present in animals?

Classification of Living Beings

All living beings are classified as below

Domain

Kingdom

Phylum

Class

Order

Family

Genus

Species

Starting from Domain to species, variations begin to decrease. This makes the theory of evolution acceptable. We cannot wholly repudiate the theory of evolution. But God shapes the design of evolution, which can be ascertained from the restrictions in the evolution of new species as detailed below. There are 3 Domains, Bacteria, Archaea, and Eukaryota, whereas there are 8.7 million species. Characteristics of all members of a species are the same. Characteristics of species of the same genus differ slightly. For example, wolves, dogs, and golden jackals belong to different species but belong to the same genus, Canis. Wolves are Canis lupus. Dogs are Canis Lupis familiaris. Golden jackals are Canis Areus. Many genera form a family. The characteristics of members of the same family differ more than those of members of the same genus, and so on. A point for discussion is why members of the same family cannot interbreed and make new genera and thereby create new species. In fact, this adaptability is highly convenient for the evolution of new species. But, offspring are only fertile if bred with the members of the same species. Of course, the only exception is interbreeding between the members of the same genus, donkey and horse. A male horse interbred with a female donkey produces Hinny, whereas a male donkey interbred with a female horse produces Mule. But a Hinny or a Mule cannot again breed and produce a Hinny or Mule. They are sterile. A horse has 64 chromosomes, and a donkey has 62 chromosomes. A Mule or a Hinny has 63 chromosomes.,. A Hinny or a Mule cannot reproduce an offspring, and they are sterile. So, interbreeding among members of the same genus itself is highly restricted, not to mention interbreeding among members of the same family, order, or class. Thus, the evolution of new species is more rigid than flexible.

If one species alters its form and a new species is formed gradually, an intermediary form must appear. We cannot cite even one example of an intermediary form. However, we may cite many examples of species being extinct. Those species that became extinct never reappear. Can we expect dinosaurs to reappear again?

So, from one-celled organisms to humans, there is every reason to believe that even if evolution takes place, it is designed by God and does not take place spontaneously. Of the 8.7 million species inhabiting the earth, why only one species, Homo Sapiens is able to dominate the earth? Why not another one, at least only one species, cannot evolve very close to Homo Sapiens in thinking capability and intelligence. Because it is designed by God, he made the Homo Sapiens the sole masters of earth.

Why Can Tigers and Lions Not Be Domesticated?

Dogs are one of the examples of domesticated animals. As per the theory of evolution, dogs wandered in the wild before being domesticated by man. If the theory holds good for dogs, why could tigers and lions not be domesticated? In fact, they can protect our homes in a better way. No thief will dare to enter our home if a tiger or lion roams around in our home. Had mankind not tried to domesticate these animals? Rich people can afford to provide non-vegetarian food for these carnivores. The reason why they cannot be domesticated is that they are ferocious in nature, and they will never lose their ferocity. Dogs are created to protect humans and their belongings. Their unflinching loyalty towards humans can never be compared with any other animal. Wolves, jackals and dogs belong to the same genus, Canis, but wolves and jackals cannot be domesticated. The food web and food chain have been beautifully designed by God. Tigers and lions cannot be domesticated, and dogs cannot wander in the wild in His arrangement.

The Brain Inside the Hard Skull

Of course, the brain is the most important organ in our body. It controls the activities of other organs, such as hands and legs and muscle movement, besides providing unmatched thinking capacity. Why is the brain placed inside a hard skull? Is it by evolution? How did the hardness of the skull, which can only be compared with the hardness of reinforced cement concrete, evolve? Why is the brain not placed in the abdomen region? God placed this vital organ inside the hard skull. Is evolution responsible for the hardness of the skull? Why are there no bones below the diaphragm protecting our abdomen? Why did bones not form in the abdominal area by evolution?! We cannot bend and touch our knees if there are bones in our abdomen. The entire skeletal structure and joints in our body are designed in such a beautiful way. The theory of evolution does not hold good in this aspect.

Voluntary and Involuntary Actions

Involuntary actions such as respiration, blinking of the eye, peristalsis and pumping of the heart defies the theory of evolution. Voluntary actions are under the control of the brain and, to be precise, the cerebrum. Activities such as eating, dancing, writing, walking and running are voluntary actions. Involuntary actions are not under the control of one's will but are controlled by the spinal cord and the hind brain's reflex action. Can the theory of evolution explain these involuntary actions? If these involuntary actions are under the control of one's will, it will not be easy to control them. We should digest food, pump blood from the heart, respire and blink our eyes. In fact, all our time has to be spent on these activities. We cannot perform any other activity except these vital functions if they are voluntary. So, God has made these activities involuntary.

The Earth-certainly Not for Humans Only

We, humans, are accustomed to think that the earth is meant for humans only. But millions of species live on the earth. Though the sixth sense is absent in all other species except mankind, they are also equally entitled to live on the earth as humans do. So, unnecessary harming of any other living being is a sin not only against the species harmed but also against God, who is the custodian of all species. It is a sin to unnecessarily uproot a plant or a tree. Practically, a question arises as to whether uprooting a weed in a field would amount to a sin. It will not amount to a sin as it is absolutely necessary to maintain a higher crop yield. Naturally, a weed will have better protection against diseases and be more drought-resistant than a crop. Weeds need less water, sunlight and nutrients than crops and are able to survive despite all odds. If the weed is not removed, it will affect the crop yield drastically. Mankind has to starve for want of food. That kind of sacrifice is unwarranted.

We, humans, must show utmost benevolence to other living organisms. Killing even a tiny creature like an ant should be avoided. Humans cannot match the endurance and agility of ants. While using animals for the utility of mankind, they should not be overexploited and harassed. But mankind is wreaking havoc on other species. Even in the 20th century, wild animals were hunted for mankind's pleasure! And for nothing else. As a result, animals develop a fear of mankind and escape at the sight of man. And, not surprisingly, birds and animals, which had not developed fear for mankind, were ruthlessly killed, and some species became extinct and completely wiped out from the earth!

Gestation and Reproductive Cycle

The period of time between conception and birth is called gestation. In the ovipary, the embryo develops outside, in an egg. Ovipary is inefficient as huge losses of eggs may occur due to predators. In some species, ovovivipary is present. In ovovivipary, the embryos develop inside eggs that are retained within the mother's body until they are ready to hatch. Ovovivipary is an improvement over ovipary. In vivipary, species give birth to young ones directly. The development of embryos takes place inside the viviparous animals. It is highly advanced over ovipary and ovovivipary. Why are these different types of reproduction? Has the theory of evolution any clue to this? Why does an elephant not lay eggs and hatch the eggs? Does the size of the species have any bearing on the reproductive method? If so, why does a tiny mouse give birth directly while a big ostrich lays eggs and hatch? Why do most birds lay eggs? Why bats, though birds, are mammals? Why and how have they adapted to become mammals? Nothing can be proved for certain. Why can't birds give birth directly instead of laying eggs? Why can't evolution improvise ovipary into vivipary? In fact, vivipary is highly efficient compared to ovipary. Birds have to fly, and it will be highly inconvenient for them to fly with extra weight during pregnancy. That is why God has arranged ovipary for them, although it is highly inefficient. How the tiny chicks get the instinct to break the eggshell to come out is another mystery. God gives instinct to every species according to their needs.

Has the size of the species had any impact on the gestation period? In humans, the gestation period is 266 days. In elephants, it is almost 600 days, and in whales, it is 500 days. In mice, the gestation period is only 19 days! In zebra, the gestation period is 360 days, in comparatively bigger bison, it is only 217 days. So, one common comparison rule between the species' size and gestation period cannot be applied universally. In kangaroo, the gestation period is only 42 days, and the calf is underdeveloped and has to be protected in the marsupium of the mother kangaroo. Even human babies are underdeveloped during birth and take almost a year to walk, whereas calves of other animals are able to walk immediately after birth. Why has marsupium not evolved in humans, though there is a dire need to foster their babies?

Generally, birds lay eggs and hatch, while reptiles, amphibians and mammals develop their offspring within their bodies.

Greed - a Vice Present Only in Mankind

Almost every species on earth lacks greed, a vice present only in mankind. The only greed present in other species is greed for reproduction. But human greed is boundless. Mankind have more greed for money than for their own life. Greed is the prime cause of all our sufferings, taught Gautama Buddha. But humankind is ready to accept any suffering to satiate greed.

Dreams

A thing we cannot avoid in our sleep is dreams. Of course, dreams appear in our sleep almost every day. Do they have any meaning? Dreams are supposedly a result of our thinking while we are awake. But, sometimes, strange dreams may occur. For example, in real life, if we see faeces, we feel nostalgic. But faeces in a dream denote good luck. If we see eggs in our dreams, it forebodes bad luck. Things that are good in real life are bad if we see them in our dreams and vice versa. Every dream has its meaning.

Suicide

The only species on earth which can commit suicide is homo sapiens. To get rid of unresolved problems, humans commit suicide. Can an elephant touch a live electric wire to electrocute and commit suicide? Or did a lion jump into a well because of its inability to hunt? Though humans think they can get rid of their problems if they commit suicide, it is a sin. Humans are created by God, and as such, they have no right to end their life on their own. Death should occur naturally while chanting the name of God. In suicide, this is not possible due to physical pain caused by suicide.

Power of Regeneration

Most of the plants can regenerate even if they are cut down. For example, if a branch of a neem tree is cut, the tree does not die. But, animals do not possess the capability to regenerate, though there are a few exemptions. The tail of a lizard grows in the event that the lizard voluntarily cuts off the tail to confuse and escape from enemies. If you cut a finger, it will never regenerate. The capability of regeneration proves that life does not reside in a particular part of the body but in the body as a whole. It also proves that the body and life are separate things. Without one another, it is not possible to sustain life.

Pollution, Climate Change and Population Explosion

Though the earth is beautifully designed by God, manmade activities are threatening the very survival of the earth. Pollution and climate change are interrelated. Air, land and water are heavily polluted as a result of industrialisation and manmade activities. Plastics take many decades to decay. People throw away used plastics recklessly. Plastics pollute land, rivers and sea. If plastics are burnt, they also pollute the air.

Climate change is threatening the very existence of mankind. Humans can adapt to temperatures 10-30 degrees Celsius. In hot conditions, a maximum of 40 degrees Celsius can be tolerated. However, an increase of every degree will result in heatwave conditions, causing a death toll. A higher quantity of water (71%)) on the earth has considerably reduced the temperature. Otherwise, the temperature should be in the range of 70- 80 degrees. Rapid increases in temperature also result in the melting of glaciers, which are perennial sources of water. Pollution caused by industrialisation and the release of greenhouse gases into the atmosphere is the prime cause of climate change.

Population explosion is another problem faced by mankind, resulting in a scramble for space, water and food. In fact, every species has the instinct, rather, greed for reproduction. Humans are no exception to that instinct. However, limited resources of the earth warrant the need for population control. God has provided the knowledge of how reproduction can be controlled. In fact, mankind has to act against the wish of God to curtail the population. The population of humans, in fact, homo sapiens, which was only 10000, restricted only to the African continent almost 2 million years ago, has exploded to 8 billion now. Had population control not been adopted, the population may be in the range of 80 billion at present! Take the case of coconut, for example. It yields many thousands of coconuts in its lifetime, spanning many decades. But it is highly exaggerated if 1% of these coconuts are reproduced. The remaining coconuts are crushed for oil. Coconuts fall just beneath the tree and lack techniques for disbursal for better survival. There will be no takers for coconut if it is not edible and does not contain oil. The economic viability of coconuts acts as a natural restriction on the increase of coconut trees, and their economic viability also acts against their extinction as the coconut trees are grown for commercial purposes; the absence of a seed dispersal mechanism is not by evolution but by the design of God.

Why God is More Benevolent to Mankind Than Other Living Things

God is always benevolent to mankind. In fact, mankind only knows the existence of God. You cannot explain the existence of God to apes. God has endowed human beings with abundant reasoning ability, which other living beings lack. So, mankind tends to revere God, and in turn, God bestows his extra benevolence to human beings, though He is the custodian of all species living on earth.

There are beliefs in many faiths regarding God's incarnation in human form. In Christianity, Jesus is the Messiah of God sent to the Earth and In Islam, Muhammad is sent by God to preach discipline and code of life among humans. In Hinduism, Rama and Krishna are considered as incarnations of God. They lived a human life on Earth.

Why Intermediate Species Cannot Be Seen

If evolution is a continuous process and new species evolve from existing species, why intermediate living beings are not seen is an interesting question. Charles Darwin himself discussed this aspect.

A Big Tree in a Small Seed

The mystery of genetics is complicated. The characteristics of a big tree are embedded in a small seed. A Banyan tree grows from Banyan seed and not a neem tree. How such vast details are embedded in a small seed is the secret only known to God.

Squirrels

Squirrels are rodents that belong to the family Sciuridae. There are many varieties of squirrels, such as tree squirrels, ground squirrels, red squirrels, black squirrels, and flying squirrels. Why and how do different varieties evolve from a common ancestor? Why and how did their colour change? How did flying squirrels evolve to jump from tree to tree? And why are the remaining varieties not as adept at jumping as flying squirrels?

Banana

Among the fruit-yielding plants, bananas are unique in that they do not have seeds in the fruits. It reproduces asexually by vegetative propagation. Its offshoots develop from the base. There are 70 species, and some of the species are ornamental and do not yield fruits. How did bananas turn to vegetative reproduction? Did the ancestors of bananas have seeds in the fruits? How and why did they gradually lose the seeds?

Moringa

In stark contrast to bananas, Moringa has seeds, but vegetative propagation is preferable. Has evolution any answer? Why does Moringa prefer vegetative propagation? Why is vegetative propagation preferred only in some plants while vegetative propagation is totally absent in most plants?

Coconuts, Palm and Dates Similarities

Coconuts, palm, and dates have similarities. They belong to the family Arecaceae. What were the properties of their common ancestor? The coconut tree yields hundreds of coconuts every year. They are used as edible and for extracting oil. The oil content is of no use in reproduction, but how and why coconuts evolved to contain oil is a mystery. The fruit of the palm is entirely different from the coconut. Dates yield fruits that are sweet. The fruit of the Areca nut is entirely different. How have different characters evolved from a common ancestor? Some of the common ancestors desired to give coconut, some desired to give palm, some desired to yield areca nut, while some others desired to have sweet taste fruits? This proves the fact that God is shaping evolution, the prime beneficiary being humans, though some animals and birds also benefit.

Fishes

An amazing variety of fishes is seen in oceans, rivers, and ponds. There are almost 34000 species of fish. Do all the 34000 species have a common ancestor? Giant whales on the one side and seahorses on the other side present different physical structures among the fishes. An electric eel can give an electric shock to its adversaries. How does the capacity of electric shock evolve in electric eels? The whole body of Lantern fish glows. Dragonfish has light organs dotted along its sides and belly. Charles Darwin himself discussed this aspect in the origin of species.

Sharks have as many as 3000 teeth set in three rows. They have a good sense of smell. Almost 1/3 of the shark's brain is devoted to detecting smells.

Aquatic Creatures

Did all the aquatic creatures have a common ancestor? Do alligators, such as crocodiles, and creatures, such as crabs, have any similarities? How did a common ancestor with some basic characters evolve into different organisms with entirely different characters?

Adaptations of Living Beings

Robber crabs can break open coconuts with their pincers. Albatross is a seabird that can sleep on its wing. They may not touch land for three to four years. They can drink seawater and have extraordinary smelling capacity. They can smell food 30 km away.

Hermit crabs borrow the leftover shell of a dead whelk or other mollusc, whatever it can squeeze into, to protect its soft body. Deep sea angler fish do not waste energy chasing prey. It has developed a clever fishing trick. It has a fishing rod with a glowing tip, which extends from its dorsal fin and hangs above its jaws. This attracts smaller fish towards the angler fish's big mouth. Brine shrimps survive in water full of salt and hot.

When ants find food, they form a chemical trail of pheromones so that other ants can find their way from the nest to the food source. Praying mantis have powerful front legs. Bombardier beetles squint a boiling, irritating liquid in almost any direction to scare away the predators. Caterpillars have irritating hairs. Ants contain a venom called formic acid.

Once the queen bee lays eggs, the fertilised eggs become female worker bees, and the unfertilised eggs become male bees. Male drones do not have stings, and their function is to mate with the queen bee. Ants also have queen ants. Ants are capable of lifting loads between 20- 50 times heavier than their body weight. They are intelligent insects, and their brain can function as fast as a powerful computer. Mozambique spitting cobra spit its venom into the eyes of an approaching person up to 3 metres away. Venomous snakes use modified teeth called fangs to inject venom into their prey. Woodpeckers have special, strong beaks that bore into tree trunks and catch insects. Gannets dive into the sea at almost 100 km/ hour to catch prey. A specially strengthened skull helps to cushion the impact of the high-speed dive. Birds which are scavengers have eyes as big as their brain. They have a poorly developed sense of taste. That is why they can feed on dead animals and rotten flesh.

Dragonflies have huge compound eyes, which cover the insect's entire head. Each one of its wings can move independently. The body of lice is flattened, which helps it lie close to its host's skin. Owl's velvety wing feathers have soft edges with fringes, which means that they are totally silent in flight. This enables the owl to swoop down undetected on its prey. Huge eyes give the owl good night vision, but its hearing is even better. The detection capacity of sound of the barn owl is so good that it can detect and catch prey in complete darkness without using its eyes at all. Peregrine can spot a pigeon flying up to 8 km away. The eyes of birds are five times more densely packed with light-sensitive cells than humans.

The silk of spiders is a protein particle. Inside the spider's body, this silk is in liquid form. Spiders have silk-producing glands and spinnerets. Sticky silk, which is secreted by spigots, secretes coarse silk to make a web. Non-sticky silk, which is secreted by spools, is a fine silk used for wrapping prey. Spiders usually weave silk during the night.

How Did Sugarcane and Bitter Gourd Evolve Their Sweet and Bitter Taste, Respectively?

Another important question is how sugarcane evolved the sweet taste. How does sugarcane distinguish itself from other grass? How did it begin to turn sweet? In fact, how is it possible for sugarcane to synthesise sugar in leaves through photosynthesis? Why don't other plants synthesise sugar? In contrast, how was it possible for bitter gourd to contain saponins and terpenoids? This is another example of God shaping evolution for the utility of mankind and other creatures.

Alcoholic Beverages

Are alcoholic beverages meant for mankind's consumption? Alcoholic beverages occur naturally. Alcoholic beverages can naturally be obtained from coconut and palm trees. Alcoholic beverages can be obtained by fermentation. Brandy, whisky, beer, rum and wine are obtained by fermentation and distillation. Brandy and wine are obtained from fruits. Whisky and beer are obtained from grains, and rum is obtained from molasses. How did fruits, grains and molasses contain alcoholic properties? Is it by evolution? Moderate consumption of these beverages helps in the reduction of anxiety. Can we assume that these beverages are meant for the benefit of mankind?

Limitations of Darwin's Theories

Darwin himself had admitted there were some difficulties in his theories. He could not believe that natural selection could produce, on the one hand, an organ of trifling importance, such as the tail of a giraffe, which serves as a fly–flapper, and, on the other hand, an organ so wonderful as the eye. He also wonders if species have descended from others by fine graduations; why don't we see innumerable transitional forms everywhere?

A great deviation, Darwin himself questioned why members of the genus proctotrupes, unlike the other members of the great order Hymenopterous insects, which are terrestrial, are aquatic in habits. It often enters waters and dives about by the use of not its legs but of its wings and remains as long as four hours beneath the surface. Yet, it exhibits no modification in structure in accordance with its abnormal habits. Why and how did aquatic habits develop in genus Proctotrupes only? This question is posing a challenge to Darwin's theory.

Darwin accepts that he himself was surprised at the evolution of the eye. In his own words," Although the belief that an organ so perfect as the eye could have been formed by natural selection, is enough to stagger anyone." Darwin explains that Landois has shown that the wings of insects are developed from the trachea, and it is highly probable that in this great class, organs which once served for respiration have been actually converted into organs for flight. In fact, the trachea is the primary organ responsible for respiratory function in insects.

Darwin could not explain the evolution of electric organs in fishes. Another case of difficulty in his theory is the luminous organs that occur in a few insects, belong to widely different families, and are situated in different parts of the body.

According to him, thorns in some species evolved as a defence against browsing quadrupeds. What prevented grasses from evolving thorns? Had thorns evolved in grasses, they could defend themselves from browsing.

He states that natural selection will never produce in a being any structure more injurious than beneficial to that being. Antlers/ horns of deer are a great exclusion to this statement. Horns do no good to deer, and they are, in fact, hindering their swift movement in the forests. Why horns had not become rudimentary through evolution is an important question.

According to Darwin, longevity is generally related to other things, mainly the amount of expenditure on reproduction and general activity. Animals expend less than men in reproduction. For example, cats and dogs expend less compared to men in reproduction. Still, they have shorter longevity than men.

The mental powers of some animals and, of course, the mental powers of man had surprised Darwin. He remarks, "Lastly, more than one uniter has asked why some animals had their mental powers more highly developed than others, such as the development would be advantageous to all. Why have not apes acquired the intellectual powers of man? Various causes could be assigned, but as they are conjectural, and their relative probability cannot be weighed, it would be useless to give them."

Here, Darwin could not explain why the intellectual powers of all organisms didn't become highly developed due to evolution, as in the case of mankind. In fact, it is the design of God. Darwin is elusive in this aspect.

Why do some insects resemble green or decayed leaves, dead twigs, bits of lichen, flowers, spines, and excrement of birds? How has evolution shaped this resemblance for the protection of insects? Darwin explains that to form such unstable modification, it is difficult, if not impossible, to see how such indefinite oscillations of infinitesimal beginnings can ever build up a sufficiently appreciable resemblance to a leaf bamboo or other object for natural selection to seize upon and perpetuate. "What is the meaning of.......for natural selection to seize upon and perpetuate?" If natural selection seizes upon and perpetuates the modifications arising in insects, who is the creator of such modifications? If an insect seeks protection from enemies or predators and thinks it is better to resemble a leaf, bamboo, or twig, can it modify itself for natural selection to seize upon and perpetuate? Is it possible for mankind to evolve into an elephant by evolution, as mankind is surprised at the massive strength of elephants? Is it possible for the elephants to evolve into mankind as elephants are surprised at the intellectual capacity of mankind? Every organism in the world is for a specific purpose. Evolution is certainly shaped in this direction and not spontaneously or arbitrarily without purpose.

Darwin's theories relied on embryological resemblances of various species. Darwin believed that the embryo is left almost unaffected and serves as a record of past conditions of the species. Embryological resemblance points the finger to the existence of an Inducer, though not definitely a creator of variations among the species and evolution of species.

Darwin came to the conclusion that it is scarcely possible to doubt that the love of man has become instinctive in dogs. There is no doubt the love of man has become instinctive in dogs. But, an important question is why the love of man is not so great in other animals. Why such an instinct had not developed in foxes or even in wild dogs? So, we may presume that dogs evolved, the evolution shaped by a supernatural force, to live along with man and protect his home.

While comparing ants and humans, Darwin pointed out that while ants work by inherited instincts or tools, a man works by acquired knowledge and manufactured instruments. The smelling power of ants is astonishing, and they can reach a place of food within minutes of placing. For example, if sugar is placed within 10 metres in the adjacent room separated by a wall, ants can reach it within minutes. But, it is impossible for humans to know the existence of sugar in the adjacent room. The agility of ants is incomparable, and they can move very fast compared to their size. God knows the requirements of every species.

We cannot deny Darwin's expression: "New species have appeared very slowly, one after another, both on the land and in the water." There is no denying the fact that new species have evolved slowly, but the design is made by God. New species evolved, in fact made to evolve, according to the needs of other species as well. For example, deer evolved to pave the way for food to tigers, lions, cheetahs, etc.; the food chain and food web are complex and designed by God. Fishes evolved to pave the way for food for sharks and whales. Grass evolved to pave the way for food for deer, cattle, sheep, etc. There is an interconnection between the evolution of various species.

Let us discuss Darwin's statement, "One species first giving rise to two or three varieties, these being slowly converted into species, which in turn by equally slow steps into varieties and species and so on like the branch of a great tree from a single stem, till the group becomes large. Of course, this is true as many genera contain numerous species. But, in the genus homo (to which humans belong), not a single other species exist on earth, along with homo sapiens! Many species of the genus homo have been said to be extinct as of now. Why in the genus 'homo' no other species is available on earth? It is the design of God to make humans (homo sapiens) supreme on earth! He does not want other species(Even in the genus homo) to compete with humans. The closest relatives to humans, the apes, belong to another genus. Orangutans belong to the genus Pogo, gorillas belong to the genus Gorilla, and chimpanzees belong to the genus Pan. Surprisingly, dolphins, which belong to the genus Delphinus, are next to humans in intelligence.

Darwin had an unmistakable belief that new species are formed by having some advantage over older forms. In a general manner, new species become superior to their predecessors . In fact, generally, it is absolutely correct. But why some species which are on the brink of extinction cannot modify and adapt to survive the hostile conditions? On the other hand, despite mankind's frantic efforts to make mosquitoes and houseflies extinct, they survive and have an unusually high breeding capacity to make human efforts to make them extinct futile. Why other fragile species cannot improve their breeding capacity to survive?

Though humans belong to homo sapiens, there are different races among mankind. How the races of Caucasoid, negroid, australoid and mongoloids evolved? There are variations of skin colour, stature, head form, hair colour, body build, nose and blood group among these races. Is there any possibility of these races turning into separate species in future?

Negroids are known for their physical valour. There may be variations in skin colour based on the climatical conditions. But how did variations in facial structure and physical valour occur? Can evolution provide any answer?

Darwin believed that animals are descended from, at most, only four or five progenitors and plants from an equal or lesser number. He also states that species have been specially endowed with various degrees of sterility to prevent their crossing and blending in their nature. He was of the view that there is some reason to believe that organisms high in the scale change more quickly than those that are low, though there are exceptions to this rule.

As species are endowed with sterility to prevent intercrossing among them and thereby restrict the creation of new species, evolution is highly restricted. Organisms high on the scale evolved from organisms low on the scale. If the change is slower in organisms lower on the scale than in organisms higher on the scale, then how did organisms higher on the scale evolve from organisms lower on the scale? If there were only four or five progenitors for animals and plants, then how do we explain the evolution of giant-sized and tiny animals and plants?

We can come to the conclusion that evolution is not by serendipity but by the planned activity of God.

References

The Origin of Species. - Charles Darwin

Book of Life -Miles Kelley

Principles of Physiology. -Robert M Berne

The Ultimate Book of herbs-Readers Digest

The Energy of Money. -Dr. Maria Nemeth

Astrology. -Carole Taylor

Salt. – Mark Kurlansky

Genetics. – S. Chand & Company

Rocks and Minerals. – Chris Pellant and Helen Pellant